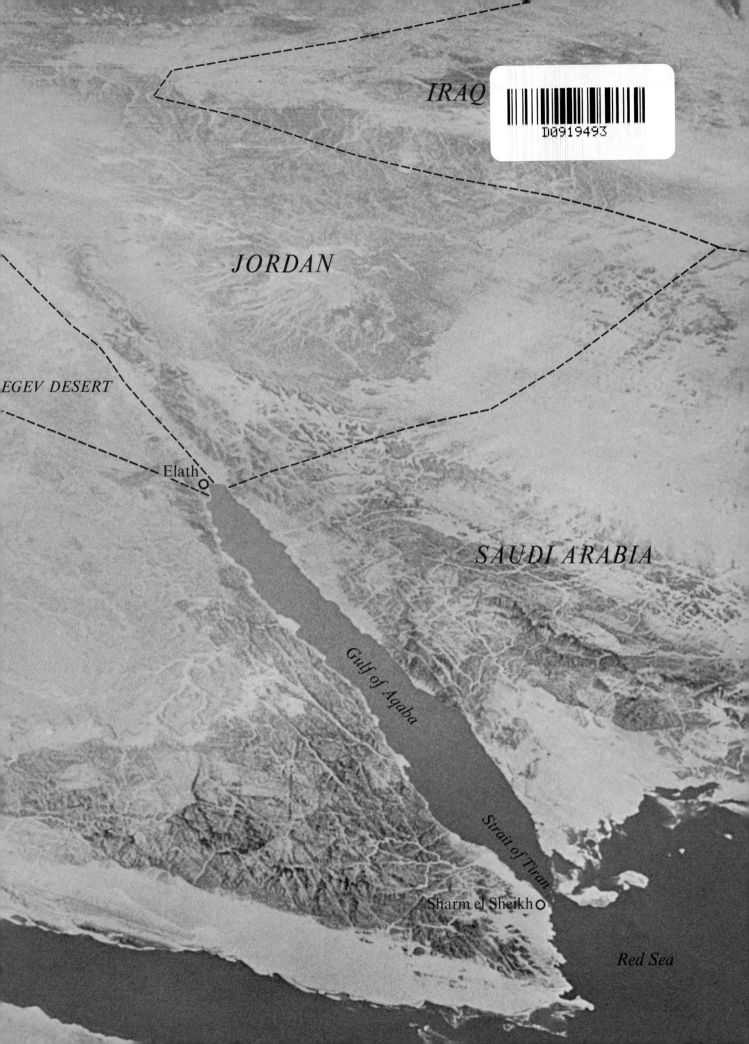

IRAQ

JORDAN

EGEV DESERT

Elath○

SAUDI ARABIA

Gulf of Aqaba

Strait of Tiran

Sharm el Sheikh○

Red Sea

SWIFT SWORD

THE HISTORICAL RECORD OF ISRAEL'S VICTORY, JUNE, 1967

SWIFT SWORD

THE HISTORICAL RECORD OF ISRAEL'S VICTORY, JUNE, 1967
BY BRIGADIER GENERAL S. L. A. MARSHALL
USAR (Ret.)
and the Editors of
AMERICAN HERITAGE MAGAZINE and UNITED PRESS INTERNATIONAL
With Pictures by Fifteen Combat Photographers Including Special Coverage from
UNITED PRESS INTERNATIONAL and MAGNUM PHOTOS, INC.

Published by AMERICAN HERITAGE PUBLISHING CO., INC.

LIBRARY OF CONGRESS CATALOG CARD NUMBER: 67-29421

Middle East Battleground

Fourteen independent Arab states (diagonal shading on the map above) stretch across North Africa from the Atlantic Ocean to the Persian Gulf. Thirteen—excluding Mauritania—are members of the Arab League. Together they constitute a loosely knit alliance united by language, religion, culture, and a common enemy—Israel.

The Arab League was born in March, 1945, when seven nations, led by Egypt, formed a political association to protect Arab interests against the rising influx of Jews into Palestine. When a boycott of Jewish goods failed to check the Zionist movement, the League sent arms and men to support their Arab brethren in the hostilities that raged with increasing intensity throughout the disputed Holy Land. After the U.N.-sponsored partition of Palestine in 1947 and Israel's subsequent fight

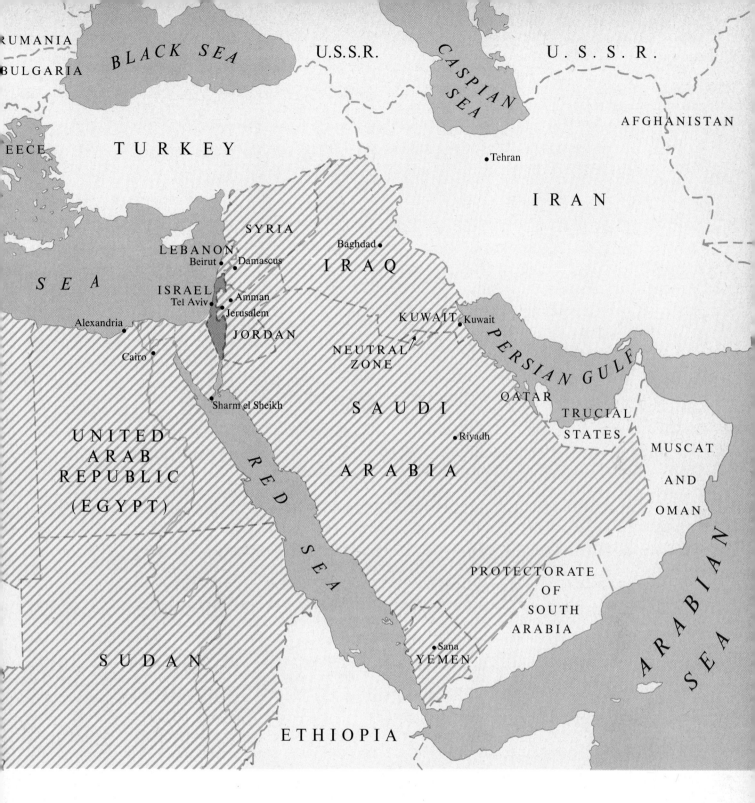

for independence, the Arabs were forced to accept an armistice in 1949—but they refused to sign a peace treaty. In 1956 Egypt's seizure of the Suez Canal triggered a second Mid-East conflict, from which Israel again emerged triumphant.

Meanwhile Arab unity had disintegrated in internecine power struggles. In an attempt to restore solidarity and at the same time bolster his own position of leadership, Egypt's President Nasser called for an Arab summit meeting in 1964. With the elimination of the Jewish state as its goal, a United Arab Command was created as a military counterpart to the Arab League. While real unity remained but a dream in June of 1967, the Arab nations nonetheless posed a formidable threat as Israel and her neighbors headed toward their third war in nineteen years.

Foreword

In the early days of June, 1967, Israel was once again fighting for survival. Its citizen soldiers were called upon to accomplish by force of arms what the Israelis had longed for since they had achieved independence in 1948—military security. Although the nation was surrounded and outnumbered by a hostile enemy that had sworn to liquidate it, in less than a week Israeli forces achieved victory in a war that stunned the world by its quickness and completeness. The army that won the war was a citizen army but it was also a modern army; its morale was high, its leadership excellent, and it was superbly equipped to fight the type of warfare it knew best, over terrain suited to a high degree of mechanization.

So swift were the events filling those six days in June that news from the ancient lands of the Middle East barely kept pace with the armored columns of the advancing Israeli army groups. To put the confused events into historical perspective, the editors of *American Heritage* and United Press International began collecting battle reports and photographs from the front and at the same time sent to Tel Aviv a man ideally qualified to piece together the fragmented story into a cohesive historical account. Brigadier General S. L. A. Marshall has been a soldier since World War I and a military analyst since the early 1920's; his book *Sinai Victory*, covering Israel's 1956 desert war, had already led him over much of the same ground, frequently in company with the same commanders. With the full co-operation of the Israeli government and the military, he visited battlegrounds where the firing had ceased only a few days earlier and interviewed field commanders while the memory of battle was still fresh in the minds of those who had fought there. His report of the action forms the bulk of the narrative that follows.

In preparing this book, *American Heritage* and United Press International were also fortunate to secure the co-operation of Magnum Photos, Inc., and particularly the work of three Magnum photographers—Cornell Capa, Charles Harbutt, and Micha Bar-Am—who were in Israel when the fighting broke out and who covered much of the action with their cameras. Their pictures and those taken by United Press International photographers comprise a vivid eyewitness accompaniment to General Marshall's text.

THE EDITORS

A young Israeli takes a breather after the first day's battle against Syria.

Glistening in the sun, the buildings of the modern Israeli city of Kinneret rise on a hill overlooking the Sea of Galilee. Only a few miles distant from the lush fields being plowed in the foreground, Jewish pioneers living in mud huts labored to turn malarial marshes into the land's first communal farm. Their efforts, at Degania, beginning in 1911, established a pattern for the development of present-day Israel.

Background to War

Israel occupies about one quarter of one per cent of the Arab lands around the eastern shores of the Mediterranean Sea. Most of its eight thousand square miles is situated in the desert, and its natural resources are meager: except for copper, no ores of any real consequence are mined there; the small quantity of oil is scarcely worth drilling for; neither stone nor lumber fit for building is indigenous to the area. A narrow strip of coastal plain provides some decent farmland, but otherwise agriculture and nature are antagonists. No river worthy of the name intersects the country, so there is no fertile river valley to yield rich crops year after year; and whatever grows in Israel grows in defiance of a hot mideastern sun that bleaches the sand, parches the earth, draws the moisture from the air, and wilts planted and planter alike.

Thus the Jews' Promised Land: the land of milk from imported cows and honey from man-planted forests—a sun-scorched, eroded, corroded country fought over, craved, prayed for, crusaded for, fiercely attacked and defended in the name of holiness since the second millennium B.C. The peoples who fight for the historic land—be they within or without its borders—invariably claim to be defenders of it, defending what is rightfully theirs; and if some law of man supports the claims of one people and not another, the unsupported cannot abide by that law. *God's* law, they will tell you, makes the Holy Land theirs. Unfortunately, no courts of law can say with certainty whether Allah's word or Jehovah's is the law of God.

To the United Nations, which was called upon to act during the violence that erupted in Palestine after World War II, one thing was certain: the Holy Land belonged to either Arab or Jew, and probably to both; but not in any case did it belong to Great Britain. So Palestine was partitioned; the 1922 League of Nations mandate that had placed Britain in charge was nullified, and the British were told to leave in eight months—by July, 1948. If the U.N. partition that virtually created modern Israel did not reduce tension in the area, it at least returned the conflict to the original, perhaps natural combatants, the sons of the sons of Abraham.

They were among the most abused peoples on earth—the Jews, descended from Isaac; the Arabs, from his brother Ishmael. For close to two thousand years the Jews had been exiles, expelled from one country after another, wandering from Morocco to Spain to Russia throughout the Diaspora (Dispersion—the term refers both to the area and to the period). But wherever they lived, Israel remained their home. The Arabs—conquered, reconquered, colonized—suffered ten centuries of no less humiliating frustration, living as perpetual subjects of foreign rule in their own homeland. While Jew yearned to return, Arab prayed for liberation. Both dreams neared fruition at about the same time, but they were irreconcilable.

Although the British were in many ways responsible for the materialization of the two dreams, their blunders nevertheless laid the groundwork for the subsequent turmoil in the Middle East. During World War I, England had asked the Arabs for help in driving the German-allied Turks from the Holy Land; in exchange, His Majesty's Government would work to establish an independent, united Arab nation. At about the same time, influential West European Jews—including the English financier Lord Rothschild—had been seeking Allied support for the Zionist cause: the founding of a Jewish state in Palestine. In 1917 Foreign Secretary Arthur Balfour declared that Great Britain was agreeable to the Zionist aim and would in fact facilitate Jewish immigration. The Turks were driven out, and the League of Nations Mandate for Palestine, assigned to Great Britain, incorporated the Balfour Declaration.

Vehemently opposed to the Balfour Declaration and to the influx of Jews, the frustrated Arabs grew angrier and more ferocious as London hedged on its promises of a united Arab state. When the rise of Nazism in Europe led to an increased number of Jewish immigrants in the 1930's, the Arabs staged protest riots, terrorist raids on Jewish communities, and in 1936, a full-scale revolt, requiring Britain to increase its troop strength in the area. The Jews responded by forming guerrilla bands for defense and counterterrorism. Fearing that the oil-rich Middle Eastern nations, which were sympathetic with the Palestinian Arabs, might ally themselves with Nazi Germany, the British mandatory government issued a White Paper restricting Jewish immigration for five years and cutting it off completely after that. The designated numbers of immigrants were calculated to restrict the Jews to a minority. The year was 1939.

During the next six years the legal Jewish Agency and the illegal guerrilla groups in Palestine ignored the White Paper and smuggled Jews from Europe to the Holy Land. After World War II, while England still refused to legalize the influx of Jewish immigrants, terrorist activity on the part of Jews and Arabs increased. At the same time, world opinion took the only turn it could as the appalling truth about Hitler's death camps became known.

World opinion and the world's new tribunal, the U.N., Zionists and freedom fighters, American Jews and the United States government, were

At Jerusalem's Mandelbaum Gate, for two decades before 1967 the U.N.-supervised transit point between Jordan and Israel, an old woman looks across barbed wire for relatives on the other side.

all instrumental in the formation of the Jewish state. But the real creators of Israel were the survivors of the European death camps. Nazi Germany's Final Solution to the Jewish Problem had been, for the most part, a success; Europe was relatively *Judenfrei*, free of Jews. Thus, when Britain took its problems to the United Nations, the U.N. was less impressed with the issues of British trade and spheres of influence than it was with the couple of hundred thousand survivors of the Nazi terror that had taken six million lives. The U.N. gave the British eight months to leave Palestine, and the Jews eight thousand square miles of the most worthless—yet to them precious—real estate on earth.

After the U.N. action but before the British departure, Arabs and Jews went at each other with a fury. Arab bands attacked convoys en route to settlements and dynamited sleeping people in Jerusalem and Haifa. The terrorist Jewish *Irgun* responded by blowing up Arab trucks and wiping out an entire Arab village. All the while the British watched, dismantling the communications centers and destroying the supply depots that the new country would need, arresting armed Jews but not armed Arabs, sending arms shipments to Egypt and Transjordan and Saudi Arabia and Syria and Lebanon, whose armies were assembling along the Palestine frontier, waiting for the British to leave. Haganah (the most cautious, and presently the quasi-official, defense unit of Jewish Israel) sent soundtrucks into Arab communities, imploring the Arabs to remain and live in the new Jewish state. Meanwhile Arab radios shrieked warnings to leave. Get out so we can come in, the Arab leaders said, in essence; as soon as Israel is destroyed, you may return. (Jewish and Arab leaders in Haifa had actually signed a truce and were discussing a treaty of cooperation and coexistence, when orders came from the Grand Mufti that all Arab families were to leave.) Close to a half-million Arabs departed from their homes; they and their descendants remain homeless still, plaguing consciences and political calculations in the Middle East to this day.

David Ben-Gurion, chief of the Jewish Agency, had said that Israeli independence would be declared the moment the British left in July, 1948. In mid-May, however, he learned that the British were planning to leave at midnight, Friday, May 14, two months ahead of schedule. Hastily he called a secret meeting of two hundred Palestinian Jews for four o'clock that Friday afternoon at the Tel Aviv Municipal Museum.

The ceremonies were brief: they had to be completed before the sun set and turned the day into Sabbath. The new Israeli Philharmonic Orchestra played the Zionist song *Hatikvah*, "The Hope," which was to become the national anthem. Ben-Gurion read an eleven-hundred-word declaration of independence and took a few moments more to announce nullification of the British White Paper. The assembly cheered, sang, and departed—Israeli nationals. The sun sank and set. Sabbath came to the Jewish state of Israel for the first time in 1,878 years.

In Hebrew lore Sabbath is the bride of Israel. This was a stormy reconciliation: by dawn of Israel's first morning, Egyptian planes had bombed Tel Aviv, and by midday all of the new nation's next-door neighbors and some from down the block had attacked. In Cairo the Secretary-General of the improvised Arab League told reporters, "This will be a war of extermination and a momentous massacre which will be spoken of like the Mongolian massacres and the Crusades." Despite the passions on both sides, the ferocity of

Above, the illegal immigrant ship Exodus *docks in Haifa in 1947, in defiance of British authority. Below, David Ben-Gurion proclaims the birth of Israel in May, 1948.*

the fighting, and the enormous difference in troop strength (Arab fighters outnumbered Israelis by a ratio of about two-and-a-half-to-one and had relatively unlimited reserves from which to draw), the Arabs were unable to destroy Israel or even to penetrate its territory very far. It was as though a violent reaction to the passivity of Europe's murdered Jews had occurred. The Israelis resisted almost insanely, destroying much with little ammunition, and even managing to keep open the road to beleaguered Jerusalem. Nevertheless, supplies were diminishing fast, and like the supplies, the unrelieved Israeli soldier could last only so long.

The Arabs, meanwhile, were not quite certain how much damage they had done, or what was holding up their thrust, or how close or far from victory they were. They did, however, know that time, geography, and numbers were on their side, and when the third U.N. cease-fire proposal arrived, the Arab command decided to accept, welcoming the opportunity to take stock. It was an enormous blunder. By accepting the truce and giving Israel a breather, the Arabs lost what was probably the only chance they would ever have to destroy their enemy without having to pay international military consequences.

The four-week truce began on June 11, and the talks, conducted by U.N. mediator Count Folke Bernadotte of Sweden, were fruitless. Israel agreed to an extension, but the Arabs did not, and on July 11 the hostilities were resumed—by the Arabs where they had been left off, but not by the Israelis. Having reorganized, Jewish forces struck out in several directions at once, quickly taking the regions of Lydda, Ramle, and the lower Galilee, which includes Nazareth. Ten days later the fighting was stopped again. This time the Arabs accepted the cease-fire, because they were on the defensive and in danger of losing the Old City of Jerusalem.

On September 17, during the period of the second truce, Count Bernadotte and a French member of the Truce Commission were shot to death by three Israelis in the Jewish (New City) sector of Jerusalem. A fair and dedicated mediator, Bernadotte was not especially popular among the belligerents, but neither could have profited from his death. The assassins were never apprehended, and their motives remain unclear.

Replacing the Count as mediator was Ralph Bunche, a member of the American delegation to the U.N. Throughout the rest of 1948 Dr. Bunche arranged, and saw violated, one truce after another. More often than not the Israelis emerged from each engagement stronger and more confident. When the Arabs launched major offensives to reverse the humiliating trend of the war, they suffered further reversals. Late in October, for example, the Egyptians in the Negev and the so-called Arab Liberation Army in Galilee began a "squeeze" offensive. Not only did the Israelis repel the advancing Arabs, they also chased and followed them into Egypt and Syria. In November and December at least three other major and many smaller Arab offensives developed into fiascoes. By early 1949 the Arab nations began to realize that the trend of war was not going to be reversed. One by one, from January through July, general armistice agreements were signed by Israel with Egypt, Lebanon, Jordan, and Syria.

The war of independence exhilarated the Israelis and humiliated the Arabs and set the pattern for Arab-Jewish relations for a generation. Little was settled. The Arabs were no more ready after the war than they had been

United Nations negotiators hold a press conference during the Israeli war of independence in 1948. Chief negotiator Count Folke Bernadotte (left) was assassinated for mysterious reasons by three Israelis, and he was replaced by Dr. Ralph Bunche of the U.S. (at right rear).

before to acknowledge the very fact of Israel's existence. Indeed, as subsequent events suggest, for the nearly one hundred million people of the more than thirty million square miles of the Arab Middle East, the tiny Jewish nation became an obsession.

The real victims, as is usual in war, were the innocent—the refugees who had left their homes, who wandered, lived in tents, and multiplied. Many had left Israel because they were ordered to do so by Arab leaders; many left because the Jews made it uncomfortable for them to remain; but the overwhelming majority left because they were afraid—afraid that the Arab invasion might fail, leaving them at the mercy of the Jews, or afraid that the Arab invasion might succeed, leaving them at the mercy of fellow Arabs who would regard them as turncoats. For whatever reason, about 419,000 left, would not go back, and wound up as wards of UNRWA (United Nations Relief and Works Agency). Opportunists in several Middle Eastern countries began forging and selling UNRWA ration and identification cards, so that a steady stream of transient "refugees" who may never have set foot in Palestine added to the ranks of the genuinely dispossessed and made the problem even more serious. By 1967, UNRWA found itself feeding about one and a quarter million Arabs.

The refugees immediately became pawns in a political contest. Most Arab nations were unwilling to accept any Palestinians, insisting that they be returned to their homes and knowing that they were unsightly symbols of the presence of Israel. Lebanon would not accept them because the refugees (mostly Moslems) would destroy the political balance achieved by that country's equally numbered Christian and Moslem populations. Syria, most affluent of the major Arab nations, did not want the drain on its economy that the influx might produce. UNRWA's Northwest Sinai Development project was intended to create agricultural communities for the refugees, but the plan fell through because Egypt would not permit the Palestinians to leave the Gaza Strip, where they were virtually imprisoned. The only Arab country that accorded full civil rights to the refugees was Jordan, but Jordan was one of the poorest Arab nations and had the most meager resources.

The Arabs who remained in Israel have become, collectively, the world's most prosperous Arabs. While the prejudice of individual Israelis frequently limits the Arabs' ability to find homes or secure employment in the cities, the official government policy has been enlightened, if not exemplary. Arabs run their own local affairs, but they do not significantly participate in the national government, and they are not accorded complete freedom of movement. Nor are they required to serve in the armed forces.

Attacks on Jews in the Arab countries during and after the 1948 war drove many Middle Eastern, or "Oriental," Jews into Israel; combined with the European Jews, they helped the young nation double its Jewish population (from about 650,000 during the war of independence) by 1952. Meanwhile, as border incidents and raids between Israel and its neighbors became commonplace, Arab resentment grew. Memories of 1948 played no small part in the 1952 Egyptian rebellion that deposed King Farouk and established Gamal Abdel Nasser as leader of the ancient country.

In many respects Nasser was a genuine reformer, sincerely dedicated to the elevation of the standard of living in Egypt. He probably had a no less sincere devotion to achieve the unity among Arab nations that had made

Above, United Nations personnel aid displaced Palestinian Arabs who fled from their homes during the 1956 crisis. In Cairo, in 1964, President Nasser and Premier Khrushchev display Egyptian-Soviet solidarity and a sleek new American car (below).

Islam a world power since the seventh century. But from the start of his tenure as self-appointed unifier of the Arab world, Nasser's rallying cry was the common hatred for Israel that Arabs shared.

Nasser also proved that he was a crafty player of international power games, balancing the Soviet Union against the United States and winning large prizes from both. But in July, 1956, the United States grew weary of Nasser's frequent anti-American actions and abruptly withdrew promised financial support for his ambitious project, the Aswan High Dam on the Nile. A week later the Egyptian ruler announced that he was nationalizing the Suez Canal, owned largely by British and French interests; tolls from the canal would finance his dam. In days gone by, England and France, which received their primary oil supply through Suez, might have retaken Suez in an instant; but these were Cold War days, and no one in the West could judge just how close Egyptian ties with the Soviet Union were. So Britain and France tried to display strength and prudence at once, sending troops to Cyprus and negotiators to Cairo and the U.N., implying willingness to yield control of the canal to an international establishment. Nasser refused to consider it, and Russia strongly supported Nasser's position. Meanwhile, the Egyptians began intensifying the activity of their fedayun, squads of raiders who crossed the Israeli frontier to attack Jewish settlements. In October, Nasser closed the Gulf of Aqaba to Israeli shipping, thereby severing Israel's only sea link with the East. At the same time the Egyptian President announced that Jordan and Syria had agreed to place their armed forces under his command.

On October 29, 1956, while Arab legions mobilized and oratory resounded across the Middle East, Israeli troops, ships, and planes struck at Egyptian targets. Mobile units rolled into the Sinai desert, and by seizing Rahfa and El Arish, separated Egyptian forces from the fedayun troops on the Gaza Strip. The strategy was eminently successful: concentrating on the Egyptians to the virtual exclusion of the other Arab powers, the Israelis sufficiently intimidated the Syrians and Jordanians, who sent not a soldier across the Israeli frontier. Despite their war talk and their superior, Russian-supplied armaments, the Egyptians were caught off guard, forced on the defensive, and routed in eight days. The Israelis captured the Sinai Peninsula and reached the west bank of the Suez Canal at a cost of one hundred eighty-one lives and one captured. Egypt lost more than one thousand killed and six thousand taken prisoner.

The Sinai war became an international crisis on the morning of November 1, when the Anglo-French forces began an assault on Egyptian air fields. Parachuting into the Suez Canal zone and advancing toward Cairo, the Europeans added nothing to the battle: they faced little opposition, for few troops were diverted to the front they had opened. Although they accepted almost immediately a United Nations request for a cease-fire and withdrawal, they actually did more harm than good to the Israelis; for the Anglo-French involvement provided Nasser with an excuse for his defeat.

The Israelis advanced to Sharm-el-Sheikh, at the southern tip of the Sinai Peninsula, from which the Gulf of Aqaba had been blockaded. As soon as the Strait of Tiran, leading to the Gulf, was reopened, Israel accepted the

When Egyptian President Nasser visited his airmen on Sinai late in May (opposite page), there was good reason for his obvious exhilaration. At his demand U.N. peacekeeping forces had been withdrawn from the peninsula; the Soviet Union had indicated support of his blockade of the Gulf of Aqaba; and Arab refugees were flocking to join the Egyptian-trained Palestine Liberation Army (below) to help in the battle to destroy Israel.

U.N. cease-fire plea, but not until March, 1957, were its troops withdrawn completely from Egyptian territory. The United Nations took over supervision of shipping through the Strait of Tiran and occupied the Gaza Strip to prevent renewed fedayun operations. Israel refused to have U.N. troops on its side of Gaza, however, for understandable reasons: almost as soon as the fighting had stopped, Nasser closed the Suez Canal to Israeli ships and announced that no ship or company that dealt with Israel would be allowed to do business with Egypt. Other Arab nations followed suit. The British government under Sir Anthony Eden fell as a result of its involvement in the war, and the United States pressured England and France not to force the return of Suez. The United Nations was not equipped to deal with any of these problems; and on paper in any case, the Israelis emerged from their triumph with a net loss of shipping routes. Thereafter, they were not well disposed to the U.N.

Scarcely was the 1956 Sinai war over when Nasser began his efforts to effect a meaningful political as well as military unity of Arab states. Early in 1958 Syria joined Egypt in the formation of a United Arab Republic, but Nasser failed to bring it off: he treated Syria as an Egyptian province, imposing his men in governmental and military positions, thereby convincing Iraq and Jordan, which had been considering membership in the Republic, not to join. From time to time the Egyptian President tried to seize power by direct

The prospect of erasing twenty years of humiliation stirred much of the Arab world to near-hysteria. In Cairo, the Volunteers for Death, a legion of Egyptians and Arab refugees (opposite page) demonstrated, calling for a jihad, or holy war. Even the old Arab below, probably witness to generations of war, was caught up in the frenzy. A cooler but no less emotional Israel readied itself: taken a few days before the war, the picture at left shows a trench being dug in front of Tel Aviv's schools and public buildings.

Just before the outbreak of war, Israeli air cadets gather under a camouflage net to listen to an address by General Mordechai Hod (between the two airmen at right) as an Hasidic visitor (left) listens in. Decorating the enclosure are pictures of air action from earlier combat with the Arabs.

force or by support of subversive elements in some of the Arab nations, which asked Great Britain for additional arms. Nasser, in turn, became more dependent on the Soviet Union and managed to leave the Middle East more disrupted than it had been before he tried to unify it. Syria seceded from the U.A.R. in 1963.

In 1965 the Arab states and Israel intensified the border skirmishes that had been going on between wars. The Israelis stepped up retaliatory attacks and struck first when threatened. A year later the Arabs began a project that would divert the headwaters of the Jordan River so that Israel would not be able to employ the power and irrigation sources of their share of the river. Miscalculations on the part of Arab engineers, the great cost of the diversion project, and frequent attacks by teams of Israeli raiders delayed and probably permanently destroyed the project.

In November, 1966, Israel reacted to Syrian border raids by destroying a Jordanian village and was censured for its action by the U.N. Security Council. In an air clash the following April, Israeli pilots downed six Syrian jets. By early May, 1967, U.N. Secretary-General U Thant was speaking of an "extremely tense and unstable" situation that could erupt once more into hostilities; Israel's Prime Minister Levi Eshkol talked of adopting "drastic" measures; the Soviet Union was secretly informing Syria and the U.A.R. of a pending Israeli attack. As tensions mounted, Nasser surprised the world by demanding on May 18 that U.N. forces withdraw from Egypt's borders with

Israel—and was perhaps himself surprised by U Thant's precipitous agreement to the demand. The Secretary-General flew to Cairo on a peace-keeping mission but returned—empty-handed—a day earlier than scheduled. Across the Middle East, mobilization orders were issued, reserves were called up, and civilian alerts were posted.

With U.N. troops gone from Sharm-el-Sheikh, Nasser announced on May 23 that he was closing the Gulf of Aqaba to Israeli shipping. The next day, in New York, the U.N. Security Council was called into what would be, for the next two weeks, almost continuous session. The American Sixth Fleet cleared for action in the Mediterranean; the Russians sent ten warships from the Black Sea through the Dardanelles to the same waters; and once-antagonistic Arab leaders flew to Cairo to sign military pacts with Nasser. The most dramatic pilgrimage was that of Jordan's King Hussein, who put his British-trained army under Nasser's command. "We intend to open a general assault against Israel," Nasser proclaimed in a speech of May 28. "This will be total war. Our basic aim is the destruction of Israel." In Israel, factories were closed as workers donned uniforms.

Meanwhile, abroad, the United Nations tried without success to devise a satisfactory solution to the deepening crisis. Great Britain and Canada suggested formation of an international fleet to challenge Nasser's blockade of the narrow Strait of Tiran, entrance to the Gulf of Aqaba. Vigorously championing that idea, the United States promptly became its only advocate, as Great Britain and Canada quickly cooled to it and then substituted the suggestion that four-power talks (including representatives from England, France, the United States, and the Soviet Union) be convened to deal with the situation. When Russia announced that it had no intention of participating in such talks, the United States again—and again vainly—tried to assemble an international armada. Israel's Foreign Minister Abba Eban flew to Paris to speak with President de Gaulle, to London for a meeting with Prime Minister Wilson, and to Washington to see President Johnson; all urged restraint—restraint while Israel's neighbors continued their mobilization on the Israeli frontier.

As May turned to June, there was some indication that the crisis had played itself out. Two weeks of gathering crisis and feverish diplomatic activity seemed to have settled into the more plodding pace characteristic of international relationships. The Israeli port of Elath on the Gulf of Aqaba, abandoned at the outset of the crisis, sat quiet and ghostlike, as though it had been evacuated years, not days, before. While Arabs rallied in their streets, hailing Nasser and demanding war, the Egyptian President sat back and waited, apparently satisfied that Israel was sufficiently hemmed in, seemingly convinced that his strategy had resulted in a major victory. It did in fact seem to a number of journalists on the scene that the conflict would be a diplomatic and not a military one. On June 3 a reporter asked Israel's Defense Minister Moshe Dayan whether he thought that the extended duration of the crisis had deprived Israel of the chance to strike swiftly and decisively, as it had in the past. "I would think," the General replied, "just now it's too late and too early—too late to react right away against the blockade and too early to draw any conclusions on the diplomatic way of handling the matter." It appeared eminently possible, that weekend, that war might not come to the Middle East at all.

*Using the French-made Mirage jets (left)
that are the mainstay of their air force,
the Israelis hit eleven key Egyptian airfields on the first day of the war and gained
air superiority at the outset.*

The Air Strike

In that least likely of all hours for achieving military surprise, between 0745 and 0815, on Monday, 5 June, when the enemy camp was certain to be wide awake if not watchful and waiting, Israel went all out to destroy the fighting power of Egypt.

To begin, her combat forces had that one aim. Most of her resources, the preponderance of her heavy weapons, were concentrated in the blow aimed toward Suez and the Nile; the Israelis had decided merely to fence with the threat elsewhere against the nation's borders.

The pressures that compelled the decision for war had been mounting for weeks. Egypt's army had massed next to Israel's borders in the Gaza Strip and had heavily fortified the Sinai Peninsula in the strength of seven divisions, two of them armored. Nasser's soldiers stood everywhere behind permanent works heavily structured in concrete. Barring all main roads into Sinai were systematically entrenched and mined hedgehogs running miles deep.

Opposite this array Israel's army had marshaled three divisions and two independent brigades. The divisions were in fact task forces of between two and five brigades each, the greater number being armored brigades, under command of a temporary division headquarters, activated for the emergency. The generals of division had been identified with their brigades only in the several weeks gone since the call-up.

Israel's justification for the strike against Egypt—the purported, immediate provocation—is on record in the words of Brigadier General Yeshayahou Gavish, chief of the Southern Command at Beersheba: "The attack of the Egyptians started with movements of planes toward Israel, which were

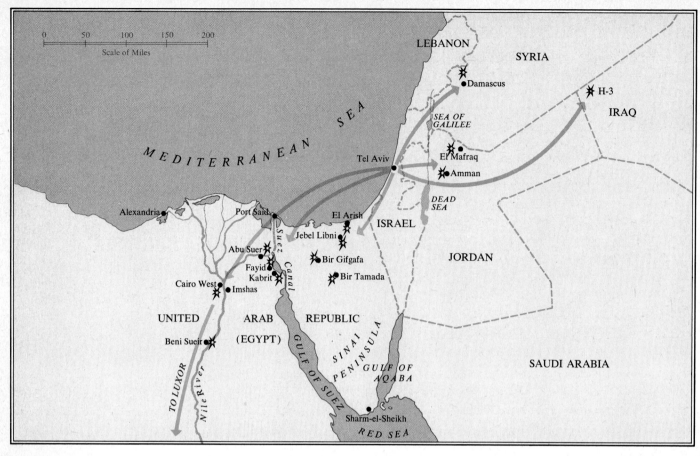

The map shows locations including: LEBANON, SYRIA, IRAQ, Damascus, H-3, SEA OF GALILEE, Tel Aviv, El Mafraq, Amman, MEDITERRANEAN SEA, Alexandria, Port Said, El Arish, ISRAEL, DEAD SEA, JORDAN, Jebel Libni, Abu Suer, Suez Canal, Bir Gifgafa, Fayid, Kabrit, Bir Tamada, Cairo West, Imshas, UNITED ARAB REPUBLIC (EGYPT), SINAI PENINSULA, SAUDI ARABIA, Beni Sueir, GULF OF SUEZ, GULF OF AQABA, TO LUXOR, Nile River, Sharm-el-Sheikh, RED SEA. Scale of Miles: 0 50 100 150 200.

Although first reports said Israeli planes hooked far west out over the Mediterranean Sea to attack Egypt, the first-day air strike was actually made as shown on the map above. The pilots zoomed in low along the Mediterranean coast and across the desert to make their synchronized attacks on the eleven Egyptian air bases (Luxor, on the upper Nile, not shown). A few hours later, other planes zeroed in on bases in Syria, Jordan, and Iraq.

detected by our radar, and with the shelling of villages along the Gaza Strip."

There is no claim that these pips on a radar grid, allegedly seen to the west over the Mediterranean, ever materialized as an air armada violating Israel's space. Of the bombardment of numerous frontier villages, however, there is adequate proof. Artillery and mortar shelling from beyond her borders was an affliction with which Israel had had to live more or less patiently for nineteen years.

When patience ended, plan took over according to a timetable that reads like the work force in an industrial plant changing shift and punching the clock. Having been told by the Army Chief of Staff, Major General Itzhak Rabin, at 0800 that the Egyptians were coming, Gavish could report at 0815 that three of his divisions were already moving on enemy territory. One column was advancing toward the Gaza Strip; the second was moving against Umm Gataf, a main Egyptian fortress organized around successive sub-ridges anchored on both sides to much higher, unflankable dunes and ridges, 30 miles southeast of El Arish; and the third division was slicing in between them, headed straight west over raw desert, roughing it where no road lay. One independent brigade was sparring toward Kuntilla in the south of Sinai with no intention of getting mauled in full-scale engagement.

To get away that fast, these several formations had to be already drawn up in march order, echeloned according to what combat would require of the columns from front to rear. They must have trained hard at it for some days; an armored division on the road stretches out twenty-five miles. Even so, the abrupt departure of these heavy columns to invade Sinai did not kill the last chance for peace-through-negotiation. That dim prospect had been scrubbed thirty minutes earlier at 0745. The further fate of the men in the desert had to be, for the anxious men at Zahal, Israel's defense establishment, temporarily a secondary consideration.

An air raid warning had sounded at 0755 over Tel Aviv, an alarm hardly portentous of where the extreme trials of that morning would fall. Not a reconquest of Sinai's armed and arid wasteland but the preserving of Israel's interior through the destruction of Egypt's air power had become for Zahal the primary, dominating objective. While the alarm went on, a radio newscaster continued his scheduled report, completed it, then on the stroke of 0800, added quietly: "We are at war." In that way some of the public got the word. Early morning in Tel Aviv was otherwise almost normally calm, except at military headquarters. The sky was bright and cloudless. Following the all-clear, men and women proceeded on their routine rounds. Motor traffic had kept rolling, disregarding the alert. Things were a little different with the children. School had recessed with the mobilization so that students could take over the tasks of delivering mail, digging ditches, harvesting, and performing other work appropriate to older hands now in military service. It was a romp to be out of school (the joy ended when school doors reopened in mid-July to make up for lost time).

So when the clock struck eight, only one thing was more certain than that a new war had come: it would not be like the last war, in 1956. After that year the balance of heavy armament in the Near East had shifted radically against Israel—through Soviet assistance to Egypt, Iraq, and Syria in the form of modern tanks and military aircraft. Arab strength in tracked fighting vehicles and mobile guns was a lesser menace, although Egypt alone could field more Stalin-3, T-34, T-54, and T-55 tanks than Israel could muster in matching armor. Dramatically altering the problem was the all-around threat from Arab air bases. They could put up enough jet bombers, such as the TU-16 and IL-28, along with MIG-21 transsonic fighters and MIG-17's, to outnumber Israel's comparable types, like the Vatour bomber-fighter and the Mirage 111C, by better than two to one. With four air bases in Sinai, two of them new, Egypt could put MIG's over Tel Aviv in seven minutes, the flight time from El Arish.

Surprisingly, for Israel, 5 June did not bring total mobilization. Somewhere between twenty thousand and thirty thousand people had not been called up. Excluded was the civil defense organization, a highly significant omission.

North of Tel Aviv at 0745 that morning there began at the several air bases a great motion and stir: crews scrambling; fighting aircraft moving to the runways, some from underground hangars; planes taking off in formations of two, six, or eight, the numbers varying according to the size and importance of the predesignated target. Such were the flight paths that farmers afield only a mile or so away might have wholly missed their going. The din and howl of this lift-off must have been deafening as group followed group low and to the west over blue water. But there was no confusion. All motion and tumult were directed toward one central purpose, little of which found echo in the nearby city. The people of Tel Aviv one month later still did not know at what time the air strike against Egypt was begun.

It was 0145 in New York and Washington when the attack order sent Israel's war planes winging toward the Nile, Suez, and Sinai—fifteen minutes before the armor was directed to roll for the borders. Those cities slept on, not knowing until 0330 that a new war was underway. By then its outcome was already virtually decided. There followed for Israel's High Command one suspense-filled hour, though not for her pilots.

First to take off was a formation of Vatour bomber fighters of the deep penetration group. Theirs was to be the farthest journey, their target the bomber base at Luxor on the Nile, far to the southwest of Sharm-el-Sheikh and almost double the distance to Cairo. The key to the master plan was this: as to Egypt, it would be a synchronized attack, directed against eleven bases only. The lift-offs were timed and staged so that each formation fronting the first wave would go at its target in the same minute. Thereafter the same eleven bases would be pounded steadily for eighty minutes. Speed had been precisely measured against distance, without the aid of computers. Having tried and tested the mechanics of the staggered take-off, the Israelis knew it could be done without fuss. There remained only the execution.

The eleven targeted fields whose destruction was expected to shock Egypt and superinduce in its air arm a state of near-paralysis were:

El Arish, Bir Gifgafa, Bir Tamada, and Jebel Libni in Sinai.

Abu Suer, Kabrit, and Fayid in the Canal zone.

Imshas, Cairo West, Beni Sueir, and Luxor in the Nile Valley.

All eleven were nominated and hit because they were the bases either for bombers or for MIG-21's, the hard core of the threat to Israel's interior. With the destruction of the fighter aircraft based on Sinai and the three fields of Suez, such MIG's as remained whole in Egypt would not have range enough to menace any city in Israel. The MIG is a short-legged aircraft.

Myth, often enough repeated, and especially when supported by arrows on a map, has a way of displacing fact. So it was that in the wake of the instant war, experts hypothesized about how Israel's airmen contrived the approach to Egypt to achieve full deception and accomplish total surprise. Most of the diagrams purporting to show the air strike have arrows indicating prolonged flight westward over the sea, then hooking back over the northeast corner of the Libyan Desert to approach the Nile from the west. Some show planes based on Beersheba hitting the Egyptian fields in Sinai.

None of this happened. There is an air base at Beersheeba; its planes and pilots supported the armored attack into Sinai from the start. All the planes in the synchronized strike that smashed the eleven main bases took off from the runways near Tel Aviv. They flew west over the Mediterranean for a short distance. Those bound for the targets along the Nile then flew on a direct southwest course to their objectives. The Sinai-bound fighters, which are certain to have staged out last because of the short distance, flew almost due south.

So we might follow along a bit with the trail-blazing Vatours heading for Luxor some minutes before anyone in Tel Aviv's street crowd even knew there was a war. They moved out over a glass-smooth Mediterranean, which, for jets moving even at subsonic speed fifty to one hundred feet above the surface, is a far less friendly sea than one a bit choppy. They had to stay dangerously low lest they be picked up by enemy radar. At that level, a smooth sea means monotony, with the blending of water and sky, the loss of horizon, incessant strain in maintaining the proper altitude, and constant vigilance to avoid disaster in the form of ditching due to a slip in judgment.

With the help of remarkably accurate military intelligence, the Israeli air force swiftly demolished a substantial portion of the Egyptian army's equipment. The shattered skeleton of an ammunition train (above) is surrounded with shell casings and other debris that remain after it was blown up by Israeli planes. At right, smoke spirals up from burning Egyptian planes destroyed on the long runways at Luxor, south of Cairo.

The pilot leading that formation, an older colonel, in civilian life a specialist in aviation, selling his wares and ideas abroad, had been on a business trip to the United States when, on 25 May, he received an informal greeting relayed by his wife: "Come home dear defense needs you." With radios silent, the 5 June formation flew on toward Egypt. During the approach, as well as in actually striking at the target, the planes flew at maximum speed, although none of the bombers or fighters flew at transsonic speed, since the war-loaded aircraft will not move that fast.

A few minutes past eight, and they were crossing the Egyptian coastline, rocketing along at treetop level. Then should have come the first warning to the Egyptians, since, from that point on, direct observation of the Israelis' passage became unavoidable. Nothing happened. Without sign of any reaction below them, the planes flew on to Luxor without incident, rose five hundred feet in the air to bomb the runways and strafe the unbunkered TU-16's, which were neatly, evenly spaced on the apron and alongside the runways. These multimillion-dollar items—twin-jet medium bombers with a range of three thousand miles and a speed of six hundred miles per hour—blazed high right where the attackers had expected to find them. At Luxor the four 30-mm. cannon on the Vatours were the big killers of Egypt's Soviet-built aircraft. Much the same sort of thing was occurring at the other ten bases by the time the farthest-south Vatours were heading for home. At Israel's insistence, the French-built Mirages and Super Mysteres had been modified to carry two 30-mm. guns instead of their original rockets. Thus, Israeli pilots beat Egypt's air force to death with cannon fire. It was so ac-

curate that correspondents credited the devastation to a new secret weapon, something that smelled out the vulnerable heart of a sitting aircraft and went right to it. To attribute what happened to the magic of expert gunnery sounded much too simple.

Thus for eighty minutes, more of the same was delivered against the seven fields in the Canal zone and along the Nile. It was judged soon after the first strike that the MIG's based on Sinai were all burned to ash and wrecked metal. There followed a respite of perhaps twenty minutes. Then for eighty minutes more, the air force went at Egypt again.

Syrian and Iraqi bases went untouched through the morning. Only twelve fighting aircraft were left at the Tel Aviv bases to defend Israel. None was put up as a screen to the north or east, and when at last that was deemed advisable, only eight took to the air.

The mastermind of this plan, without doubt the greatest gamble with the largest payoff in the history of military aviation, sat in his unpretentious command post at Tel Aviv, supremely confident that it would work. At age thirty-nine, about one year earlier, Brigadier General Mordechai Hod had taken command of an air force that weight-for-weight was probably the most effective fighting machine anywhere, made so largely by his predecessor, Brigadier General Ezer Weizmann, now Deputy for Operations. Weizmann shaped the tools and trained the men. Hod was the man with the big idea.

Hod belonged to the first class of pilots ever to win wings in Israel, this on 14 March, 1949. A third-generation Sabra (native-born Israeli), he had taken his first flight training in Czechoslovakia in 1948, then converted to jets in England. Married, the father of three children, this chief is anything but a martial type, despite his trim figure and erect bearing. A warm man, given to gentle humors, with a twinkle in his eye, especially when he speaks English as if he were not quite sure of himself, he participates keenly, agrees enthusiastically, and disagrees fairly. Hod would be good company in any circle. There is not a bit of side to him. He deals with people as if he enjoys them.

There were some simple reasons for his conviction that he could win the battle for Israel over Cairo. He calculated that it would take the Egyptians one hour to assess what had happened and a second hour to agree on what could be done about it. He was convinced that when hit, they would not tell the truth to their allies. Instead, they would proclaim a victory, disarming in its effect. Syria and Iraq he could not take seriously; they were just an inconvenience. But he made one mistake. Instead of a lag of two hours, the Egyptians gave him four hours. Long before that it was all over. The planes of the first wave had all returned to home base by 0900. It was then that Hod put up the screen to the north. By the time the operation had been going for two hours fifty minutes, or at approximately 1100, he was able to report to Minister of Defense Moshe Dayan: "I am certain that there is not another bomber left in Egypt."

Yet he did so like a man walking in a dream. His intellect told him that his calculations must have worked out. His emotions simply refused to accept it. It was something too big for acceptance by his whole being at one time. Not until the following morning did it become matter-of-fact, past and proved.

Beaming at his desk, General Mordechai Hod (left)—behind a model of one of the fighters that helped win Israel's stunning air victory—receives a message of congratulation for his brilliant military planning.

During the days of strain before war's outbreak, as he braced for the problem, Hod had been almost alone in his high optimism. His political superiors, and some of the generals, looked askance. The plan was too bold; should it fail, ruin could result. They attributed its venturesomeness to the impetuosity of youth, which Hod at two-score took as a left-handed compliment.

Whereas people may ask if Hod is a genius, simplicity is his favorite word, the key to his system. He believes that modern air power has become oversophisticated; there is so much gadgetry that too little time is left for relentless schooling and practice in the fundamentals. His average pilot on that day was twenty-two and had begun his training in jets at eighteen, as a high school graduate. Making the pilots' shooting more precise was a simple instrument Hod and his people had devised to keep the target in frame, an instrument they substituted for a French-made electronic wonder that came with the plane, rejected because testing proved that one factor had been overlooked. It was another simple calculation that at 0800 the Egyptians at the eleven air bases would have taken a break for a spot of tea. Leaving unscathed Egypt's additional fourteen bases was reckoned a safe enough risk by General Hod.

Knowing by 1100 that he had won the air battle in Egypt, Hod began shifting bombers and fighters to Sinai to support the attack by the armored columns. Around noon he began the air attack on the bases of Jordan and

The tourist attractions of Egypt, long denied to Israel's citizens, were viewed from a startling new angle by Israeli pilots on the morning of June 5. Above is the Sphinx, as photographed from an Israeli plane en route to bomb Egyptian airfields in the Cairo vicinity. At right, three smashed MIG's line a runway at Imshas.

OVERLEAF: *Two Mirages come in low (left and upper right) over the Jordanian capital of Amman to bomb industrial-military targets on the city's outskirts.*

Text continued on page 32.

Syria and continued it through most of 5 June. But they were in effect finished after one hour. The only Iraqi base strafed was H-3, along the pipeline, just east of the border of the Jordan panhandle. One squadron of MIG-21's had set down there just in time to go out like a light. Habaniya, near Baghdad, was not attacked, being beyond range of Israel's bombers.

A third or more of Nasser's war planes remained in condition to fight. Well aware of it, Hod had no intention of renewing the assault on the bases. There had been no dogfights; not one MIG had risen to challenge a Mirage. So Egypt's pilots would always have an excuse for themselves: "We were given no chance to show what we could do." If their morale was to be shattered irreparably, it would have to be done in the air east of Suez. So here was the implicit invitation to come on and try. The air-to-air dueling started that Monday afternoon somewhat west of the Bir Gifgafa-Jebel Libni line and continued into Tuesday. There were growls and gripes from Israel's soldiers fighting below when the MIG's first appeared above them. Hod heard rumbles like this: "Look, you said you destroyed their air force; it's still around." Until cured, it had to be endured. Egypt threw SAM missiles into the air fight from the park west of the Mitla Pass, a fact that went unreported. There are entries in the record; an Israeli pilot said casually: "Hey, one of those blazing telephone poles is after me." No harm was done by the SAM's; Israel's fighters were flying too low.

Some of the story is told in statistics. Hod's people flew only 492 sorties to kill 402 enemy planes on the ground. All told, Israel's forces destroyed 452 planes; some were gunned down by antiaircraft batteries. There were thirty-one dogfights near Suez and above western Sinai; five Egyptian planes were shot down, not one Israeli plane. Hod lost twenty-five pilots, twenty-four of them when their ships were shot down by ground fire; the other man died as a forward observer with the army. Yet the 492 sorties were the lesser part of the work load; airmen flew nearly a thousand sorties in support of the armored advance into Sinai.

Hod was above all elated by the performance of the Fougas. The Fouga Magister, built in Israel, is the basic trainer for jet pilots, and this relatively slow schooling craft had been souped up with two machine guns and thirty-six rockets to operate as a tank-killer over Sinai. Older men—El Al pilots and others from civilian life—had been called back to man this fleet. These turtles of the air force destroyed more than seventy Egyptian artillery pieces, took on the enemy armor wherever they found it, and softened the base camps before the armored spearheads came up. Their over-all contribution to quick victory is incalculable.

Hod learned that he had sorely underestimated the resources of his men and their machines. He had expected three to four sorties a day from the average pilot; he got an average of seven, and some went as high as ten. He figured the standard of gunnery established in peacetime training would drop during combat; instead, it rose. He anticipated that the serviceability of aircraft would slip steadily downward once fighting started. To begin, it was ninety-nine per cent, and it held that way through six days.

One young pilot shot down four enemy planes. In between number two and number three he was hospitalized for a wound, then ducked back to duty without permission. But for the wasted time, he might have become Israel's first ace.

1. לפני הפגיעה

2. בפגיעה

3. אחרי הפגיעה

A sequence of photographs taken from a camera-loaded Israeli fighter shows the destruction of an Egyptian fighter plane.

32

Israeli Chief of Staff Itzhak Rabin and Defense Minister Moshe Dayan hold a press conference during the first weekend in June, 1967.

The blow dealt Egypt by General Hod's men and machines on the morning of 5 June doomed President Nasser's hope for any military success against Israel.

Defense Minister Moshe Dayan, himself a dirt soldier, was quick to point out that decision was never in doubt thereafter. So there *was* something new under the sun: for the first time, air power had effectively won a war.

It remained for the armored columns under General Gavish driving forward in Sinai to confirm and consolidate a military victory virtually in hand. The luckless Egyptian formations trying to defend the eastern desert had become trapped between the upper and nether millstones.

Yet no one had planned it that way. Knowing the challenge would come sometime, Israel's military did not respond to it by extracting from the secret files a paper with force levels, targets, supply loads, and maneuvers—all tabulated and charted, drawn to regulate all men and all motion. There was no such paper.

Zahal—the defense establishment—knew how it would proceed in a general war against any Arab combine that included the U.A.R. It would knock out Egypt first; for if Egypt collapsed, the others would fall. Therefore Sinai had to be the main theater, and the army, already pointed westward, was trained and schooled with the requirements for fighting there uppermost in mind.

Certain brigades became highly specialized in precise knowledge of the terrain and all possible routes for military movement. Maps and photos of the peninsula preoccupied them. Soil experts, archaeologists, and other scientists were consulted about the possibility of moving around dunes and across badlands where seemingly not even camel caravans had traveled. The premise was that to conquer Sinai swiftly, it would have to be done with armor. Israel's army got to know the possibilities of Sinai far better than the army that stood there.

Much of this was the doing of Brigadier General "Rab" Yariv, Israel's G-2, as scintillant an intelligence brain as serves any nation, and unlike most of the breed, a positive thinker and talker. Yariv, formerly Israel's military attaché in Washington, fits the term "a gutty little squirt," so slight of body that a wind would blow him over, so big in nerve that a whirlwind would not try. Everybody calls him Rab, which is short for his nickname, The Rabbit. Talk boils out of him like bullets spitting from a machine gun. It is invariably to the point, as when, past mid-May, the crisis deepening, higher authority asked him: "How much time do we have to win a war? [Before the U.N. or the Big Powers would intervene.] What kind of plan should it be?" Yariv replied: "Minimum forty-eight hours, maximum ninety-six hours. Better plan for a two-day war."

So Israel in early May had no elaborated design for quick victory. There is adequate collateral proof that what came had to be crash-planned, the expanse and weight of the Arab threat not being foreseeable. But Israel knew what was out there, in fighting formations and fortifications along her borders as May opened, and in the augmentation of both as May lengthened. Yariv's system made it possible. Later Dayan gave him public credit: "We had almost perfect intelligence." One exception was at Rahfa. The massive buildup there had occurred too late in the game.

Over the ten years since the Israelis had left Sinai in 1957, the peninsula had been methodically fortified, according to the Russian idea of how to make the desert impregnable to armor. All main approaches, and some less obvious, were blocked by concrete works and deeply ramified trench systems, revetted with masonry of rock or straw-mud brick. As May, 1967, came, Egypt rested on the works and forces already garrisoning Sinai. They were:

—2nd Infantry Division, with organic armor, each brigade having one armored battalion, with one battalion of tanks and one of tank destroyers directly under the higher command.

—Two brigades of the 20th Palestinian Division, with about forty tanks in the Gaza Strip.

—1st Armored Brigade.

—Two mobile reconnaissance battalions, numerous units of Border Guards, and a logistical establishment ample for fielding a full-size army. All told, there were not more than two hundred fifty tanks in Sinai.

There were now four airfields, two new ones having been built since 1956 —a minor one at Jebel Libni, a large field for jets at Bir Tamada. Three fighter squadrons—one of MIG-17's, one of 19's and one of 21's—were based on the peninsula. New roads had been built to support and supply the airfields through south-north movement, a new branch highway led to Mitla Pass, and there had been added a paved east-west highway to the Suez Canal, midway between the long-existing central routes.

There was nothing in this for Israel to feel particular alarm about, and no alarm had been taken.

Syria, which throughout the winter had nettled and harassed Israel's border, thereby exacerbating Middle East tension, had only three brigades

Brigadier General "Rab" Yariv, right, head of Israeli army intelligence, explains his army's movements in Sinai to S.L.A. Marshall.

in line on the commanding ridges of the Golan Plateau overlooking Huleh Valley and the Galilee region. This great rampart, a natural battlement of black volcanic rock, had been so garrisoned since 1955. The brigades lived in bombproof galleries under the rock. The fire trenches on the military crests of the ridges were walled with the same rock. Pillboxes of concrete added strength. Tunnels connecting installations on the reverse slope with the fighting line were roofed with concrete and loose rock five feet thick.

Here were the strongest works in the Middle East, and behind them an army of such indifferent quality that Israel had not reacted when, in mid-April, Syria began to mobilize reserves. The regular army had ten brigades formed in three and a half divisions; the mobilization had put 240,000 Syrians under arms by 1 June.

Jordan, too, was heavily fortified at all possible points of ingress along the common border with Israel, although there were no corresponding defensive works on Israel's side. The Jordanian army (once called the Arab Legion) was formed of nine infantry brigades, one mechanized brigade (the Royal Guards), two independent tank brigades, and five artillery battalions, one with Long Toms, two with self-propelled 105-mm. howitzers, and two with 25-pounders. The tank brigades were shaped around two hundred M-48A1's (Pattons), obtained from the United States, and one hundred forty M-113 armored personnel carriers, there being an armored infantry battalion with each brigade. The weapons had been partly paid for out of United Arab Command funds. Jordan had further one battalion of M-47 tanks and one of Centurions.

In early May all this artillery was, as usual, already deployed along the ridge lines of the West Bank, the guns positioned to fire on Israel. Of nine Jordanian infantry brigades, only two were east of the Jordan River, as was the mechanized brigade, this screen stretching as far south as Aqaba. The two tank brigades were in the Jordan Valley. Seven infantry brigades were west of Jericho, manning the trenches and strong points along the rim of the bulge, except for the one brigade concentrated in Jerusalem. These were routine dispositions; Israel had learned to live with them without running a fever.

Thus early May was as near normal as any that Israel's citizens and their armed forces are likely to know. There was no apprehension of a pressing and palpable large-scale danger.

The first inkling of something possibly stirring came in the week preceding 15 May, Israel's Independence Day. Messages went from the Kremlin to Damascus and Cairo; the Soviets said they possessed "hard" information that Israel was preparing to attack Syria. Since there was nothing of the kind intended, Zahal thought it interesting, though not alarming. Then on 14 May, Egyptian Field Marshal Fawzi went to Damascus, and the visit was widely publicized.

The next day—Independence Day—Nasser started moving reinforcements into Sinai. In Tel Aviv this displacement of forces out of Egypt was interpreted as an attempt by Nasser to wring political profit out of a show of force. Other Arab leaders were calling him a do-nothing; he could claim that the push into Sinai had the object of deterring Israel's rumored strike against Syria. But it was still a charade unless he could get rid of the United Nations Emergency Force. This is how men reasoned at Zahal.

Eight days before war erupted, Arab members of the Palestine Liberation Army in the Gaza Strip clean their weapons for the expected easy conquest of neighboring Israel.

After that, Fawzi wrote U.N. General Rikky, telling him that he must move aside. Secretary-General U Thant thereupon intervened, replying in effect: "Any such demand should be addressed to me. If the U.A.R. makes such a demand, it has that right and privilege." Israel's intelligence reckoned then that the fat was halfway in the fire. U Thant had left an opening that Nasser could not ignore if he were to keep face. Left no choice, he had to get rid of UNEF.

Phase 1, or the twilight of the crisis, lasted from 15 May until 23 May. Israel, still wondering how far Nasser would go and whether anything would be done from the outside to restrain him, was already started on a partial mobilization. But the nation's leaders still hoped that nothing more dire would come of the crisis than added stress on an already strained economy. A number of commanders who figured conspicuously in the war were not recalled to uniform until the final week of May. The day of no return, when the second phase of the crisis opened, was 23 May. With the closing of the Strait of Tiran by Nasser, Israel's General Staff began to function with the intensity of a body already at war. That was when the planning conferences began to make the specific decisions that gave form to the air battle and the invasion of Sinai. Mobilization could be built upward more gradually and without friction because the Arab confrontation was already present. In fact, Nasser had done Israel a favor by making the threat clear beyond doubt. Israelis in uniform were braced and steadied by his maneuvering. Still, nothing of consequence was done to rearm toward Syria or Jordan. Syria was unimportant. Even when King Hussein went to Cairo and signed the pact, Jordan was not expected to take the plunge.

The reasoning went like this: Nasser must be so impressed with the might of Soviet arms at his disposal that he anticipates a *fait accompli* from the build-up, a bloodless victory, with Israel yielding. In this illusion, Hussein joins him.

By 23 May there was more than enough Soviet-made hardware in Sinai to nourish the wishful thought. Following Independence Day the build-up of enemy numbers was not more impressive than the haste. The order of battle in Sinai by 1 June counted seven full divisions. They were: 20th Palestinian Division in the Gaza Strip, now complete with organic armor and artillery; 7th Infantry Division, between Rahfa and El Arish, in the last stage of assembly; 2nd Division at Umm Gataf and Abu Agueila; 3rd Division at Jebel Libni and Bir Hasne; 6th Division along the Kuntilla-Themed-Nakhl axis; 4th (armored) Division around Bir Gifgafa and the Wadi Meliez; the division-size Task Force Shazali (named after its general) in the Wadi Kauraya north of Kuntilla; and finally, two independent armored brigades, 141st in Jebel Libni and 40th at Bir Hasne.

A reinforced brigade, with allied attachments, had been at Sharm-el-Sheikh since the Strait of Tiran was closed. It had not dug in or in any way improved the position, another item in proof that Nasser expected to win without a fight.

The Egyptian infantry divisions numbered twelve thousand men, the armored, eight thousand. Thrown together, they were an unwieldy mix of old regular brigades and cruder reserve units put on a war footing because of the trouble in Yemen. Throughout, however, their armor, artillery, mortars, and 240-mm. Katusha rockets (there were two battalions so armed) were the latest Soviet models. Nine hundred or more tanks had been deployed. Many Russian-made supply vehicles showed less than a thousand miles on their speedometers. All signal equipment was first-class. What else, other than this array, could have emboldened Nasser to say: "You wish to fight me, Israelis? OK, come along"?

On the Golan Plateau, where three brigades had been in the front line, by 1 June there were three more, two of them in reserve positions. Backing them up were two division-size groupings, with one infantry, one mechanized and one armored brigade in each, along with a full complement of artillery. Altogether, sixty thousand armed men had been put forward by Syria between Damascus and the border.

Jordan stood-to approximately as earlier described, as ready as Jordan could be, not needing to shift forces to increase the pressure short of war. The heavy armor in the Jordan Valley would then be more useful in the high ground north of Jerusalem.

The vise around Israel had clamped a little tighter by the time Hod struck. The net effect of this bit of stengthening was to enlarge the wastage of forces. The columns of armor now charging into Sinai made certain of that.

Still, the Egyptians in line awaiting them had no reason to believe they faced an army already heavily advantaged. By noon on 5 June, Israel's high command knew that the blow in the early morning had wrecked Egypt's air force. Still, no claim was made. Twelve hours passed before there was an official statement on this subject. Wise or not, it seemed better not to let the enemy have the information, although Jordan might have taken one step forward, then three to the rear if King Hussein had known at once. Besides, to contend against Radio Cairo's extravagant claiming was in any case impossible. Thus the fellaheen in a fighting suit in Sinai that day, if he tuned in on a voice from Cairo, heard words like these: "Welcome to the jihad waged to recover Palestine. Your eagles, my brother soldier, shot down twenty-three aircraft. Brother, haul down the flag of Israel in Tel Aviv."

Former rivals for power in the Arab world, Egypt's President Nasser (left) and Jordan's King Hussein embrace in Cairo as they meet on May 30 to pledge unity against Israel.

The Arab town of Gaza, at the eastern end of the Gaza Strip, was officially surrendered to the Israelis on Wednesday, June 7. That morning a convoy of about twenty Israeli tanks and half-tracks moved through Gaza's nearly deserted streets (left) to flush out what remained of the Palestine Liberation Army.

The Sinai Campaign

The invasion of Sinai was planned at General Gavish's Southern Command headquarters in Beersheba during the days immediately preceding 5 June.

The army commander expected that the battle would run at least one week. Much less certain than General Hod that absolute command of the air would be won in the first hours, Gavish did not count on it in making his arrangements. Should the air strike succeed wholly, then good. If not, his three divisions would do their attacking by night to save lives. The estimate was that the battle for Sinai would cost at least five hundred men.

He knew that the Egyptians had first-class tanks and artillery, but he believed that the gunners would be ill-trained and indifferent marksmen. He did not know his opponent, Lieutenant General Murtaji, who had just arrived at Bir Tamada to command Egypt's field army. The chief weakness of the Arab force in Sinai, Gavish felt, was that only four hundred of the nine hundred tanks deployed there were with the two armored divisions.

One threat in particular bothered him. Under interrogation, Egyptian prisoners who had blundered into Israel's lines by night said that a main effort would be made to cut through the Negev east of Kuntilla. Elath was defended by only two battalions, and only one brigade was stationed along the border near Kuntilla. Opposite it, deployed along the passages of the Wadi Kauraya was a large special force of Egyptian armor, which, since 31 May, had been led by General Shazali, a commander well regarded for his performance in Yemen. The Arabs had twenty Centurions at Kuntilla, elsewhere T-54's and 55's, one hundred tanks altogether. By penetrating between Mitzpeh Ramon and Elath, the special force could cut across Israel and link up with the Jordanians.

Although their advance strafing had cleared many Gaza streets, the Israeli Army's Wednesday morning passage through the town was tense. Pausing for a smoke but not a rest, the soldier above scans shuttered windows for snipers.

Although the Egyptian threat to the Negev was a nagging worry, it was still small compared to the over-all question that concerned Gavish: could Israeli armor break through strong Arab fortifications built up over ten years? The details of how it was to be accomplished, position by position, were worked out during the last days of May. On being named Minister of Defense, General Dayan did not alter the plan. He inspected immediately—insisted on his right to do so—looked over the troops, studied the arrangements, and liked what he found.

On 5 June, starting at 0600, the Egyptians began shelling twelve Israeli settlements along the border next to the Gaza Strip. At the same time, Gavish got a call from the commander of the independent brigade near Kuntilla; Shazali's forces were moving toward him across the desert. The Israeli field army had maintained radio silence for fourteen days, all nets being closed. After Gavish received his order to start the attack, at 0745, it took his people fifteen minutes to get the nets going again. At 0800 he gave his order.

The immediate effect of the order was to launch three division-strength columns of armor against Sinai, with the Suez Canal as their general objective. In the south the independent brigade would try to stall the eastward movement of Force Shazali and thereafter simply fence with it, not having the power to risk full-scale battle. Another independent brigade stood by, not far from the northern border of the Gaza Strip, ready to attack the city of Gaza when Gavish gave the word. From the beginning Gavish sought,

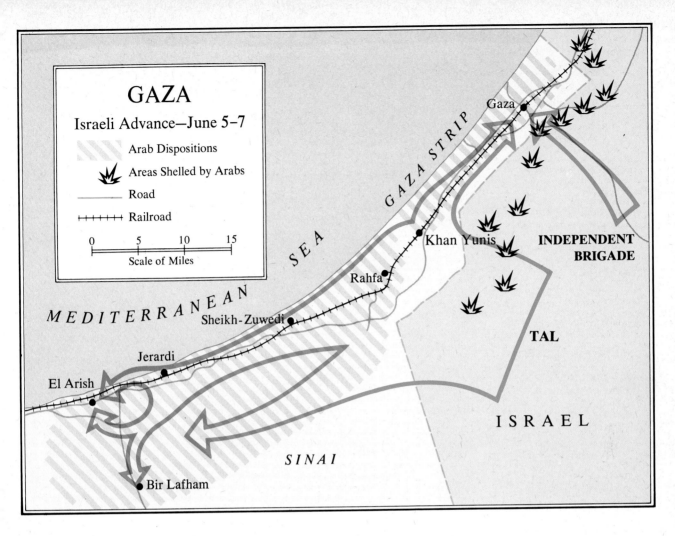

GAZA
Israeli Advance—June 5–7

Arab Dispositions

Areas Shelled by Arabs

Road

Railroad

0   5   10   15
Scale of Miles

GAZA STRIP

Gaza

MEDITERRANEAN SEA

Khan Yunis

Rahfa

Sheikh-Zuwedi

Jerardi

El Arish

Bir Lafham

SINAI

INDEPENDENT BRIGADE

TAL

ISRAEL

first, to destroy Egypt's army, and second, to establish a dominant position at Sharm-el-Sheikh and the Strait of Tiran. These things could be done, the General Staff reasoned, only by taking the whole of Sinai.

As swiftly as he could break free of his own headquarters at Beersheba, Gavish moved to the forward command post of the division already attacking westward along the coast. The main trials of the first day, 5 June, were certain to occur there.

Facing Division Tal at the western end of the Gaza Strip, extending eight miles north and south, was a wall of solid positions, gunpower, and men. The Egyptian 7th Division had deployed its three brigades in line, parallel to the main highway where it bends south out of Rahfa. Thereafter the Arab line ran straight west to El Arish. Two additional battalions were based east of Rahfa, short of Khan Yunis. Behind the infantry front was a full brigade of artillery. West of the artillery base was the great hedgehog, Jerardi, a fortified position blocking the main road for six miles from east to west. Within it were thirty bunkered tanks, mainly Shermans, and several thousand troops. Composing the array was a full division, plus two brigades; one hundred Stalin-3 tanks were in line just behind the front of zigzagged fire trenches. Mine fields forward of the trenches varied from thirty to two hundred meters in depth, and other mines were planted between the perimeters of the several brigades. Antitank batteries, mounting six to twelve guns in each stand, were distributed fairly evenly along the front. They were emplaced in pits,

The northernmost Israeli attack of June 5 was directed against Egypt's Gaza Strip, a narrow stretch of coastal land cutting into Israel's western flank (map above). It was here that Egypt, having ordered withdrawal of the United Nations peace-keeping forces, had begun to amass troops, shelling Israeli border settlements, and increasing the provocation for war. On Monday morning, as other Israeli tank columns moved out to engage enemy forces in the Sinai Peninsula farther to the south, Division Tal moved into the Strip, taking Khan Yunis and Rahfa. By June 7, Israeli forces had gained control of the Gaza Strip and were pushing westward through El Arish along the coastal road to the Suez Canal.

with barrels just above ground level and the embrasures concealed by grape-vines. From Rahfa, one artillery battalion pointed south to deliver crossfire.

Division Tal had no intention of driving head-on against this formidable front; that could have proved fatal. Instead, the Israelis planned to send a brigade of armor, and two battalions of paratroopers serving as armored infantry, to probe for the open flank to the south. This force would move through the dunes, then penetrate between the infantry trenches and the artillery base.

Directing the entire operation was Brigadier General Israel Tal, chief of Israel's armored force. Forty-two years old, short but not stocky, Tal is a dynamo, so aggressive in conversation that he keeps it one-way. A farm boy from Beer Tuvia, he is a genius on the mechanical side. As a lad, he built himself a submarine, tried it in a slough into which the neighborhood sewage flowed, and nearly drowned. In the British Army he was an expert machine gunner who gained distinction by making several improvements in weaponry. He has raised Israel's armor to zenith by concentrating on gunnery rather than movement. "If we shoot well enough, the other side will have to move," is a saying among Israel's tankers. Given a chance to study at Hebrew University some months ago, Tal chose philosophy. His hobbies are astronomy and the conquest of space; he is a nut on these subjects.

The evening of 4 June Tal had fretted and at the last moment changed his plan, with Gavish's approval. Instead of striking first at the 7th Division's

right flank, he would throw two tank battalions straight north across the border toward Khan Yunis.

The two battalions—Pattons on the right and Centurions on the left—jumped off from the Wadi of Shalilah at 0815 on 5 June, straight for Khan Yunis, five miles away. Crossing the border at 0845, they withheld their own fire and were not fired upon. This first stab into enemy country would have proved as untheatrical as a staff ride, except for one thing; as the tanks raced on, the colonel in command heard a voice speaking Arabic on his channel. "What does he say?" he asked a linguist in the tank crew. Came the translation: "They come. They are on us. Two great columns of dust. What can we do? What can we do?" The Egyptian answer was given in five minutes. All the Arab artillery around Rahfa opened fire. But instead of barraging the two approaching tank columns, these guns resumed shelling the Israeli settlements, because they were set that way and no one ordered a change. Tal's columns ran on, the Centurions holding to the main road, the Shermans on the right crossing over planted fields. The pincers pulled together in the center of Khan Yunis—the run completed without one shell being fired. But the tanks did not stop there to mop up; they attacked toward Rahfa. The news of the quick capture of Khan Yunis was the first heartening word to Israel.

Colonel Uri Baron of Moshav Orot is a brigade commander who had taken over a battalion of Pattons because of the supreme importance of the first blow against the 7th Division front. Still pondering what line would best

Anxious to secure the town swiftly and move southwest down the Gaza Strip, the Israelis were periodically slowed by Arab sniper posts, well equipped with machine guns, grenades, mortars, and bazookas. The Israeli soldiers on the opposite page, nearing such a post, cautiously approach the blue Egyptian jeep to their right. But as the close-up photograph above reveals, the jeep contained no threat: the holes in the vehicle suggest that the Arabs manning it had been killed earlier by Israeli machine-gun fire.

serve the assault, Baron was well forward. The fact is that Israel's army did not have an accurate reading on the main Egyptian defenses; the works around Rahfa had been built only during the previous four or five weeks. Although Jerardi had been fortified for almost five years, the depth of the positions along the highway to El Arish remained a puzzle. The General Staff reckoned that resistance along the Rahfa line might run into the second day. To attack it by night would require too many infantrymen; thus it was decided to strike by day with armor.

While Baron and his tankers looked on, waves of Israeli-built Fougas, flying very low, came on for a thirty-minute strike with rockets against the artillery base. These planes had been placed directly under Gavish's command. The Egyptians put up a storm of flak, but it was a perfect strafe, and not one Fouga got hit. The air force, destroying two thirds of the field pieces based near Rahfa, made two hundred sorties on 5 June in support of Tal.

Baron's Pattons then ran forward, seeking the soft spot south of the mined front. The Fougas roared back to pound the guns again as the tanks came even with the defended line, so that there would be no interval between the shock dealt the artillery and the attempt to breach the infantry positions. The company commander stood in the turret of the leading Patton. The tank hit a mine and exploded into flames, killing both captain and crew. Their deaths saved the others. The tankers that followed saw at once that the captain had made too short a turn. Guiding on the pyre, they swung farther south through the dunes before veering west, then north, on a hook around the entrenchments.

Trailing after the tanks, using the same lane, came the armored infantry in half-tracks. Already the movement started to fall apart. The armor was charging on to strike deep and finish off the artillery positions. The infantry was to double back and assault the main trench line from the rear. Traversing the loose dunes, however, the half-tracks simply could not keep the pace. Engineers had the mission of clearing a lane through the mine fields.

Completing the destruction of the artillery, the armor engaged a battalion of Stalins, destroyed most of them with gunfire at short range. A bit giddy with their success, both battalions ran on to attack infantry and machine-gun emplacements farther west. That was a mistake and not according to their instructions; one battalion was supposed to turn and help the armored infantry in its mop-up of the entrenched line. The fog of war was thickening and General Tal realized he was in trouble.

After neutralizing some of the positions on the Egyptian brigade farthest south, the paratroopers of one battalion had moved on north to attack the central perimeter. At that point their luck ran out. They became isolated and immobilized by fire on the ground where the two brigades joined.

Getting a call for help, Tal first bombarded the Egyptian brigade in the center with all his guns. He next dispatched his reserve infantry battalion to follow in the tracks made during the opening assault and to fight through to the beleaguered force. The other battalion of paratroopers had gone on to Rahfa to engage the garrison there. Tal ordered it to forget Rahfa for the moment and turn south to help relieve the encircled battalion. The battalion of armor that had careened on was directed to reverse and carry out the mission as planned. The result was much superfluous motion, with none of Tal's quick-fix improvisations working out as he planned.

44

If speed is critical to Israeli offensive strategy, so is rest. Characteristically, the soldiers above drove without pause for more than forty hours. Then, before dawn on Wednesday, they wrapped themselves in blankets, lay down alongside their half-tracks, and slept their first sleep of the war. At left, Israelis who had entered Gaza the night before prepare to leave. One soldier recites his morning prayers while facing the town police station —formerly the headquarters of the Egyptian military command.

Colonel Baron's tanks had already blasted the six battalions of 122-mm. and 100-meter artillery pieces, as well as the 85-mm. and 57-mm. antitank batteries, to complete the destruction the Fougas had begun. Baron now heard the distress calls and the new orders on his command radio. His Pattons were close to the scene. (All the tank commanders had been instructors at the Israeli school for armor, and their students now formed the tank crews.) With his battalion well collected and in the right place, Baron decided he must move to the rescue, though uninvited. From the rear his tanks destroyed the greater part of a brigade of eighteen hundred men. The fight to save the isolated battalion lasted ninety minutes, ending around 1700. Fifty of the Israeli paratroopers were dead.

The armor that had dashed through Khan Yunis was now moving toward the Sheikh-Zuwedi position; the reserve battalion was making a sneak run for El Arish on a track through the dunes well south of the highway; and the armored infantry was mopping up Rahfa. At 1900, as darkness fell on Monday, 5 June, Tal moved up to the crossroads south of Rahfa to talk with several battalion commanders. Artillery, mortar, and machine-gun fire churned up the ground around them. Then Tal realized for the first time that the Egyptian brigade farthest south had not been wiped out. Twenty tanks and one half-track of paratroopers, reinforced by two lieutenant colonels, commanding battalions, were launched on an attack against the brigade. After brisk, brief fire from the moving vehicles, the greater part of an Egyptian force of twelve hundred surrendered. There was no time for a mop-up.

Sometime after 1900, Tal got the stunning news that the battalion of Centurions that had sideswiped Khan Yunis had raced through the Sheikh-Zuwedi and Jerardi fortresses, traveling the main road, and was idling along the eastern edge of El Arish. Tal wasn't prepared for this; the enemy obviously had let the battalion have free access, intending to close the trap from behind. Next he heard that the Sherman battalion out of Khan Yunis was lagging far to the rear, that the Egyptians had swung the gate closed at Jerardi, and that the highway was being heavily shelled.

Out of his reserve brigade, Tal ordered one battalion of tanks and one of armored infantry to drive to the west and attack the Jerardi fortress from the flanks. The Israeli artillery was advanced to shell the position and keep it illuminated. At midnight Tal heard from both battalions that they had become stuck in the dunes. He and his staff still lingered at the Rahfa crossroads. The armored infantry battalion fighting in Rahfa was ordered to disengage and form on Tal. The battalion commander was given a quick briefing on the position and the situation; he was then directed to move out over the coastal road and assault Jerardi from the front. As the fight started, Tal got the word on radio that the battalion of Shermans had broken through Jerardi and joined the Centurions.

Once again, the fortress had opened the door only to close it. Tal now had two armored battalions isolated at El Arish. That left him no option but to throw everything else that the division had against Jerardi. Jerardi's fortified belt, extending six miles along the highway, almost two miles in breadth, was anchored north and south on unflankable dunes. The dunes as well as the flat ground were entrenched and fixed with concrete pillboxes and strong points. All along the six miles, bunkered-in tanks were positioned to fire on the highway.

The fight for Jerardi lasted ten hours. The highway had been left solid and was not mined at its eastern end. Tal's tanks bulled their way along it with fire, then squared off to enfilade the trenches. The armored infantry mopped up these diggings with Uzis and grenades, then stormed the strong points scattered along the dune crests on both flanks. Though tedious and exhausting work, it proved to be not too costly. Many of the Egyptian tankers fled before taking a hit or firing a round.

The division front arrived at El Arish, and without taking the town, broke through its center with a platoon of Shermans. The tanks then were set up as a roadblock to the west. Tal had this block in place, sometime after dawn on Tuesday, with one brigade deployed along the eastern edge of El Arish. Most of his forces were still strung out, fighting, all the way back to Khan Yunis. The brigade trying the secondary route along the southern edge of the dunes had temporarily foundered somewhere in the sand sea. The battalions—tank and infantry—that had attacked the front of the Egyptian 7th Division were *hors de combat* and in no condition to move. Tal had left them during the night and had advanced his command post, via the coast road, to El Arish. He sent a message to the reserve brigade: "Rest up, reorganize, and protect yourselves."

El Arish was ignored for the moment. The troops up front skirted the

Brigadier General Israel Tal

Egyptian army officers, such as General Munam Abdul Husaini, Military Governor of Gaza, were inclined to surrender with absolute military propriety. At right, erect and in full uniform, he stands in an Israeli half-track carrying him to an interrogation point.

OVERLEAF: *An Israeli convoy, en route to the Sinai interior after capturing El Arish on June 5, passes a truckload of Arab prisoners being taken to the rear. To clear the desert track, disabled vehicles have been shoved to the sides.*

A desert dawn silhouettes Israeli infantrymen giving an enthusiastic send-off to an armored column at Nitzana, jump-off point in the Negev for the thrust into Sinai.

eastern side of the town and headed straight for the air base. Bedlam greeted them. Ammunition trains loaded with katusha rockets were exploding, the earth was quaking, and artillery was blasting from the south. A battalion of Stalins came on in a half-hearted attack over the runways. Four of the Arab tanks were destroyed at a distance of a half-mile; the others turned and fled south to the Bir Lafham hedgehog—another large fortification not unlike Jerardi. The Israeli battalion that had been crawling along the dunes appeared at 0700 Tuesday. Tal sent it to attack positions east of the airfield.

Hard fighting continued at Khan Yunis and Rahfa that morning. Tal, at El Arish, still had no idea how badly his division had been hurt. Officers were being hit right and left, but no one bothered him with the bad news; the second-in-command took over and kept going. In one spot he had lost five tanks within five minutes, all killed by mines. Still, no one bothered to tell Tal. Much later he found out that the first twenty-four hours of battle had cost him seventy dead, thirty-five of whom were officers. More than one hundred twenty-five wounded had been returned to the rear; he did not know about that either. Earlier he had published an order that said to all his men: "Armies in other countries in other wars could afford to lose the first battle, and then apply the lessons of defeat. We are different; the cost of losing is too high. So it is life or death. We think only of decision; we don't think of losses."

The order had been heeded all too well. Hugging the illusion that he had lost less than fifty men, Tal at El Arish still decided that he would have to be more careful. Despite the size of the Bir Lafham position, he put only one battalion against it. It was made up largely of "tank snipers," gunners who are so expert that they rarely miss. He told them: "Proceed with a fire fight at long distance." They engaged the enemy from flat ground at three thousand meters, and over that distance they killed sixteen dug-in antitank guns and six Stalins. The brigade commander then advanced the tank battalion and at the same time loosed one company on an outflanking move eastward along the dunes. Tal saw it move out and thought the idea so good that he threw another battalion into the assault. It shelled the trench system from in front while the moving force on the dunes took it line by line in enfilade. Lasting two hours, the maneuver virtually collapsed the Egyptian defense; Tal did not lose a man or a vehicle. To finish the thing off, he mounted on tanks a battalion of armored infantry to barrel straight down the pavement running through the center of Bir Lafham, shooting up the trenches on both flanks. He went along in his command car, trailing the battalion commander, who rode in a half-track. Halfway along, a T-55 tank, firing only its machine gun, drove straight for the Israeli half-track; the fire set the half-track ablaze, and five men were wounded. Other men from this same section jumped aboard the T-55 with grenades and killed the crew.

From east of El Arish, another half-tracked battalion of infantry attacked the city in early morning. A house-to-house fight developed. By 1000 on Tuesday, 6 June, all resistance ended. Thereupon, Tal reorganized, and the division moved out in two directions. One task force of armor, self-propelled artillery, and infantry drove west along the coastal road. Thirty miles west of El Arish it collided with a block of six M-55's, backing up entrenched infantry. The fight lasted through Tuesday afternoon. On the following morning, however, the column reached the Suez Canal. Meanwhile, Tal's two brigades that had come forward to El Arish were sorted out south of Bir Lafham for movement to Jebel Libni.

Along the western end of the Gaza Strip, around Rahfa and Khan Yunis, the fight went on. Tal's reserve brigade, reconsolidated there, was grappling with a local resistance that the armored battalions in their rush had not mopped up. Gavish threw his independent brigade into this struggle, and Khan Yunis was taken all over again. The two brigades then separated, one to strike for Gaza from the western end of the Gaza Strip, the other to go against the city from the east, after first attacking the Egyptians positioned along the commanding ridge of Ali Muntar. The force out of Khan Yunis—a battalion of AMX light tanks and several paratroop companies riding in half-tracks—took on the 20th Division of the Palestine Liberation Army, strong in armor and supported by three artillery battalions. The Palestinians resisted stubbornly; the fight lasted two days. Although Ali Muntar had fallen before midnight on 5 June, the cost of taking it was high. Eight AMX's had their bottoms blown out and most of their crews killed by mines. Gavish realized too late that this was no place for light tanks and withdrew them. The paratroopers fought on. At 1200 on Wednesday, 7 June, the Israelis, with large help from the air force, took Gaza. The price of the drive through the Gaza Strip to the city was sixty dead and more than two hundred wounded. Gaza and Rahfa were the bloodiest battles of the war.

Division Yoffe had cleared the way for Tal's brigades heading south, and they had plain sailing to Jebel Libni. When the column turned west on Wednesday morning, one brigade fought a brief action at El Hamma against entrenched Egyptian infantry supported by SU-100 tank destroyers; the brigade did not lose a man. The task force on the coastal road was even then fighting its last battle before taking Kantara and the bridge at Firdan.

Approaching Bir Salim, Tal switched another brigade up front. He knew that the Egyptians still stood in strength around the air base at Bir Gifgafa, and he ordered the fresh brigade to occupy both road intersections to the north of it. He then sent to the west one company with fifteen AMX's to serve as a blocking force. As the brigade went into defensive position at the crossroads, it was attacked by two Egyptian battalions of T-55's. From the air base, Egyptian artillery shelled the positions, and four MIG-21's flew in low and bombed the brigade.

Worn down and more satiated than satisfied, Division Tal's main body drew up within range of the airfield for a rest, leaving the blocking AMX's out on the limb. At midnight sixty T-55 tanks, coming from the west, collided head-on with the fifteen Israeli light tanks that had formed as a laager enclosing the company's thin-skinned vehicles. There was mutual surprise. In the opening exchange of fire, two Israeli AMX's were immediately destroyed. The two leading T-55's tried to swing wide around the right flank of the laager. The first was hit broadside, but the shell did not penetrate; the second took a round in its magazine, and the explosion blew the turret from the hull. Two more T-55's moved up, firing. One round hit an ammunition-loaded half-track inside the laager. The chain reaction from the explosion blew up every other half-track, destroyed one AMX, killed twenty men, and

In a four-day thrust that broke the back of Egypt's military power, Israeli infantry and armor swept across the Sinai westward to the Suez Canal (troop movements shown on map at right). At 0800 on the morning of June 5, General Gavish, head of the Southern Command at Beersheba, gave the signal to advance in a three-pronged attack across the desert: Tal in the north through El Arish along the coastal road; Yoffe due west to join flanks with Tal, later blocking the Mitla Pass; Sharon to drive for Umm Gataf. An independent brigade pointed toward Kuntilla would block the Egyptians under General Shazali, who threatened to cut through the Negev to Jordan. On June 7 Israeli torpedo boats and paratroopers took Sharm-el-Sheikh and broke the Egyptian blockade of the Strait of Tiran. By June 8 the Israeli army had reached the eastern banks of the Suez Canal, and by nightfall the entire Sinai Peninsula was under Israeli control.

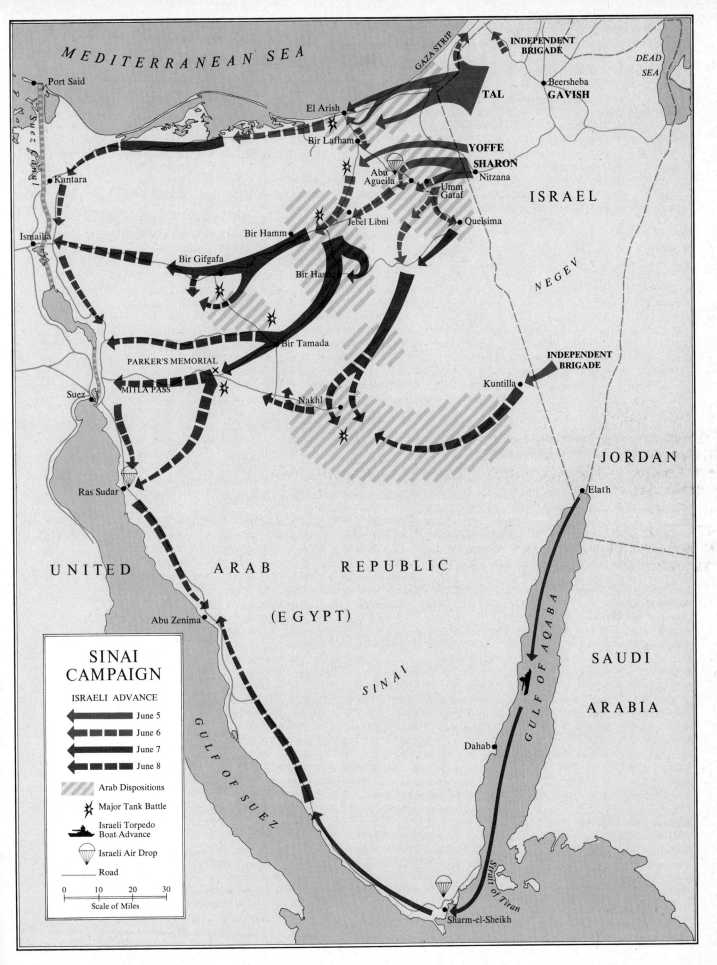

MEDITERRANEAN SEA

Port Said

Suez Canal

Kantara

Ismailia

Suez

El Arish

Bir Lafham

Abu Agueila

Umm Gataf

Nitzana

Jebel Libni

Quelsima

Bir Hamm

Bir Hasne

Bir Gifgafa

Bir Tamada

PARKER'S MEMORIAL

MITLA PASS

Nakhl

Kuntilla

GAZA STRIP

INDEPENDENT BRIGADE

TAL

GAVISH

Beersheba

YOFFE
SHARON

ISRAEL

NEGEV

INDEPENDENT BRIGADE

JORDAN

Elath

DEAD SEA

Ras Sudar

UNITED   ARAB   REPUBLIC

(EGYPT)

SINAI

Abu Zenima

GULF OF SUEZ

GULF OF AQABA

SAUDI

ARABIA

Dahab

Strait of Tiran

Sharm-el-Sheikh

SINAI CAMPAIGN

ISRAELI ADVANCE

June 5
June 6
June 7
June 8

Arab Dispositions

Major Tank Battle

Israeli Torpedo Boat Advance

Israeli Air Drop

Road

0   10   20   30
Scale of Miles

wounded many others. In a minute the commander at the disaster point was on the radio calmly reporting to Tal what had happened. Tal said: "Try to fall back one kilometer." All the division's artillery was loosed to cover the withdrawal. The T-55's pulled back from the fire. One company of Shermans went forward to help extricate the AMX's. The company came to the wreckage, charged on, and engaged the T-55's, killing five of them. The others withdrew westward. The brigade nearest Tal was ordered to move out, pass the AMX's, and strike for the canal. The second brigade, which had been sitting on the crossroads, was turned south to attack the airfield. These things happened around dawn of the fourth day, Thursday, 8 June.

But the brigade with orders for Suez (forty miles away) had to refuel and was slow in getting away. Tal then ordered a company of Centurions to drive on past the AMX block and to be prepared to spar if the M-55's struck eastward again. One half-hour later, Tal was having coffee with the brigade commander, who suddenly said: "The Centurions have gone too far; they're out of radio range." Alarmed, Tal replied: "Speed on up there and pull them back." Some time later the commander called to Tal on radio: "I was too late; the company commander is dead." The Centurions had cruised on, looking for a fight and finding it. Thirty M-55's had come against them, and the cannon had destroyed ten of them. Near the end of the fight, one 100-mm. round from a T-55 hit the top of the tank where the captain stood, wrecking the turret and killing him. A second Centurion was totally destroyed by two armor-piercing rounds.

Along the axis of Division Tal on the run into Suez the Egyptian tankers did not quit. The tanks were bunkered hull-down on both sides of the road in undulating ground. They could see the Israelis come on as they topped one of the distant rises and were ready when they came to the last of them. Finally understanding what was happening, the brigade commander put tank snipers forward to scout out this hidden armor and engage it from longer range. At eight hundred to twelve hundred meters, the Israeli shooting was accurate, and the Egyptian firing was not. The Egyptians changed tactics. The tanks quit the bunkers and pushed out to the dunes on both sides of the road to harass the column from the high ground. To checkmate this new move, the Israeli brigade also changed tactics. Two tanks advanced astride the main highway. Several hundred meters behind them came sixteen tanks in an L-shaped half-box, its base spread evenly on both sides of the road. Through the dunes, three thousand meters to the north, another platoon of Israeli tanks advanced in column. Too far away to fire, this distant wing, by threatening envelopment, gradually collapsed the Arab resistance along the main highway. On the road to Suez the brigade destroyed another one hundred Egyptian tanks, of which sixty were T-55's.

By nightfall on Thursday, Tal had two spearheads on the Suez Canal and was preparing to join them. They were being worked over by Egyptian artillery from the far bank of the big ditch. One of his tanks was knocked out by an antitank rocket—the Shmel.

During the advance from Rahfa to the Suez Canal, Division Tal lost 150 men killed and 620 men wounded. Forty of the dead and seventy of the wounded were officers. The division claimed to have destroyed upward of 275 tanks while losing fifty. Tal felt disappointed only in himself. He had had too little to do. The men and the junior leaders had carried the burden.

General Ariel (Arik) Sharon's over-strength division moved out at 0815 on 5 June from the neighborhood of Nitzana in six columns spread over a ten-mile front. The desert along that section of the border is not too formidable. Riven by many small ravines and spiked with table-top hills that stand alone, it is not dune-strewn.

Like Yoffe, Sharon had never commanded armor before. In common with Tal and Gavish, he was basically an infantryman and had specialized as a paratrooper. Thirty-eight years old, a family man, Israel's Director of Training, Sharon in the field, as along all other paths, is hard-charging, a difficult man to work with, and as sure of himself as was the late General Patton, with the same fire and temper. Tightly self-disciplined, he gets much out of men, though not through love.

Under him were two infantry brigades and one of armor, an extra tank battalion, one battalion of engineers, and six battalions of artillery. In the field an Israeli brigade, like a U.S. division, is self-sufficient, with its own services and supply enabling it to fight alone. Although the armored brigade has fewer men than the infantry brigade, the figure three thousand can be taken as an average. Half the division was standing force, half were call-ups from the reserve.

One mile beyond Egypt's Sinai border the division front swept past the entrenched mesa Auja Masry, until recently a United Nations Emergency Force watch post, which had been abandoned. On the horizon to the west rose Tabat Umm Basis, Egypt's forwardmost defended outpost. Sharon's advance guard hit it shortly after midday, and from there on his troops were skirmishing against delaying positions east of the fortress of Umm Gataf, Egypt's strongest position in Sinai. Six miles away was Abu Agueila, the linchpin of the enemy front.

They knew what they were up against before they started. Westward were two main bodies, ten miles apart. At Queisima to the southwest were four Egyptian infantry battalions, seven of artillery, and ninety tanks. Directly ahead, within the entrenched and supposedly unflankable hedgehog organized around the sand ridges of Umm Gataf were four battalions of infantry, six of artillery, and about eighty tanks. Sharon was not yet worrying about the further enemy strength that lay beyond, deployed along the line Bir Hasne–Nakhl. If he could overrun Umm Gataf, he would do all right and so would the rest of Gavish's army advancing toward Suez. The center of this moving front was on the high road—the solid-enough paved right-of-way that runs from the Israeli border to Ismailia on the Suez Canal. Somehow the parallel columns breaking trail across the wasteland managed to keep pace fairly well.

Northernmost was a special task force under Sharon, following a serpentine track through a sea of sand dunes. The mission of this force was to go straight west for twenty miles, pass the highest dunes that bound Umm Gataf to the north, get on the El Arish–Abu Agueila main road, and prepare to hit the village and the fortress from the rear. In that way, if the main body was held up by the mine fields and guns of Umm Gataf, resistance could be collapsed by penetration from the west. In this task force were one battalion of tanks, a company of armored infantry, one battery of 120-mm. mortars, a platoon of engineers, and other small elements. For the men of the task force, nothing was easy. There were two defended Egyptian positions along

Brigadier General Ariel Sharon (left) arrives at the battle-front via helicopter.

55

the way, the last one covered by a battalion of infantry and twenty tanks. Three lines of trenches, anchored on high dunes and extending more than one mile in depth, were a formidable delaying obstacle. There was an afternoon-long fire fight before the Egyptians were outmaneuvered.

This was a bitter fight, the worst blow taken by the division during the daytime jousting with the outposts. In the first round, the task force lost one company commander killed, three platoon commanders killed, and two company commanders wounded. Seven tanks were lost, mainly to mines. The task force recoiled, and while it was trying to gather itself, a sandstorm, lasting more than two hours, fouled all weapons. At 1500, the commander tried again; this time, helped by an air strike from eight Fougas, the column tried to outflank the position on the right. It was knocked back again. A distress signal was dispatched to Sharon, who sent his operations officer by helicopter to have a look from above. From his perch, he saw a route by which the bruised task force could swing far to the right through the dunes and circle the Egyptians' mined front. Going that way, the force emerged on the El Arish road at 1730 and immediately got into a running battle with another strong enemy force. This was truly the hard-luck outfit.

Sharon's columns farther to the south were spread out, both because of the strength and expanse of the Egyptian front they were attacking and because of the almost foolhardy complexity of the plan that Sharon had approved to collapse it. In all, his plan embraced five separate movements, all but one of them convergent and all having to be regulated at night.

Umm Gataf lay twelve miles west of the border. The heaviest column advanced on the main highway straight toward it. South of it another column struggled along on what is called the Turkish Road, over firm but rough and rock-strewn ground, a track so bad that those who travel it keep to the way only because the going on either side looks far worse. Dunes hem it in.

Still farther left of these main forces, in which the tank battalions fronted for the half-tracked armored infantry, a reconnaissance grouping veered off sharply to the southwest. It was made up of one company of AMX light tanks, one company of infantry in jeeps, one battery of heavy mortars, and an engineer platoon. The group's task was to get astride the road running northwest from Queisima, block it with a defended perimeter, and stop the Arab garrison there from counterattacking toward Umm Gataf.

East of Umm Gataf, in the several outposts, the Egyptians had placed not more than two rifle companies and about twenty tanks. All were eliminated by early afternoon. A halt to the general movement was called, while the central column still lay several leagues east of Umm Gataf. The division had to collect itself. Its slowest element, the line infantry brigade, could not walk from the border and there were no army trucks available; thus it was coming forward slowly in city buses. From each company of armor Sharon sent one tank forward to reconnoiter. These scouts stood off from Umm Gataf's eastern defenses at fair shooting distance, and through most of the afternoon, exchanged fire occasionally with guns inside the position.

From where they stood, they could not see it all. The hedgehog was roughly five miles deep by three miles wide. The entrenched flank to the south was anchored on a lofty and impassable line of rock ridges, while on the northern side the sea of dunes closed right down to the relatively flat and fortified ground. Between the two-hundred-meter-wide mine field that covered

By Thursday, June 8, the Israelis had reach the east bank of the Suez Canal, in the vicinity of Port Said. Arab stragglers in this part of the Sinai desert had little choice but to surrender. Fortunately for them, however, the town of Kantara, the only agreed-upon prisoner-exchange point, was nearby. In all probability, the Egyptian being frisked by an Israeli soldier at right was on his way home by Sunday.

Although the Israelis were engaged on three fronts, their conquest of Sinai was quicker in 1967 than when they had fought only against Egypt in 1956. At right, the victors' tanks race past Arab corpses just thirty miles from Suez.

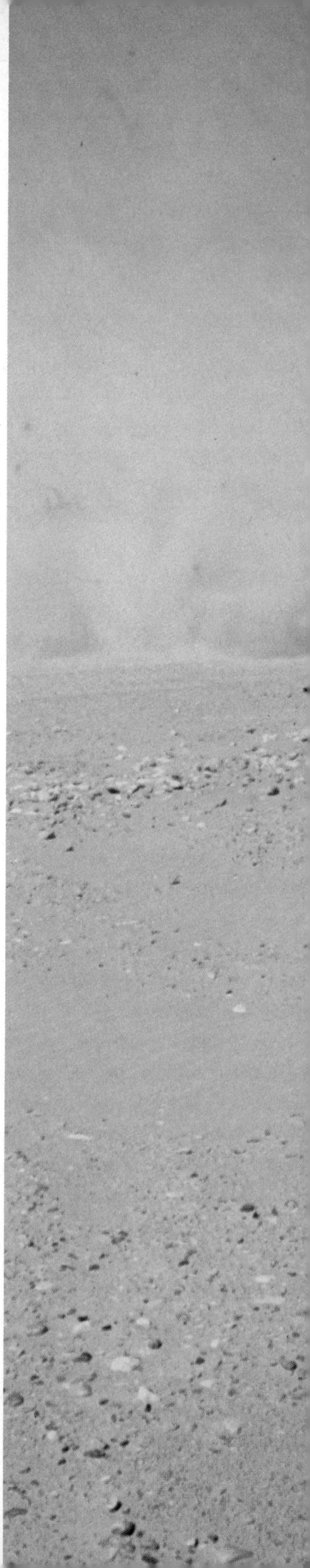

Umm Gataf on the east and the village of Abu Agueila to the west were three main trench systems. Scattered in between were multiple secondary works, such as concrete pillboxes with machine-gun nests and bunkered-in tanks with their guns pointed east along the road. There are fifty-foot-high sub-ridges running at right angles to the road throughout Umm Gataf. Their crowns are fixed with good trenches, dug when the British were present in the Middle East. The Egyptians had manned them in 1956. But since then, the Russians had changed things. The main trench systems were in the low ground, level with the road. More curious still, on the outer side of the mine field to the east (there was another to the west where the column that had swung north around the dunes lost six tanks later in the night) there were no entanglements or barricades, but only a single strand of barbed wire. The mines were of plastic and had been made in Communist China.

To breach and break this most elaborate of all fortifications in Sinai, Sharon had prescribed the following movements:

After dark, the infantry brigade would attack the enemy's left flank, getting there by a forced march halfway up the slopes of the dunes. As he reckoned it, that halting advance through the loose sand would go on for about ten miles.

Reaching the objective, the brigade would enfilade the nearest trenches, then turn back east to "open a gate" for the engineers at the north edge of the mine field. From the inside the engineers would then clear a lane through the mines where the highway ran so that the armor could come on through.

After dark also, a battalion of paratroopers would be set down on the dune-tops out of S-58 helicopters. They would head west to overrun the artillery base and destroying the six battalions. Sharon figured it would be a two-mile walk for them; it proved to be four.

As such things go, especially in night operations, this was a Rube Goldberg design. Either it would be brought off at all points or it was likely to fail everywhere. Confined to the road, the tanks had to have free way, which meant that the clearing of the mines and the killing of the artillery had to be certain. Even to get his own artillery in position to fire effectively, Sharon had to capture the front of Umm Gataf very early. His guns were already as far forward as they could get to pound the trenches nearest the mine fields; after registering, they ceased fire.

By 1800, with one hour of daylight remaining, the infantry brigade had marched west along the dunes and come under artillery fire. After a brief rest, the men marched on at 1900; by radio their commander gave Sharon an estimate that it would take him until 2230 to come opposite the hedgehog and begin the attack out of the dunes.

General Gavish flew in by helicopter at about this time. He wanted to be beside Sharon during the main battle. At his command post the Chief of Staff, General Rabin, was having second thoughts about the over-elaborated plan. He got Gavish on radio, to say: "Maybe we should put this thing off till tomorrow; it's pretty tricky; we could then use air force; it might save

Brigadier General Yeshayahou Gavish, chief of the Southern Command at Beersheba.

many lives." Gavish said: "No!" Then he put it to Sharon, who also said: "No!" Nothing had yet gone wrong, and it was a little late for change.

At 2100, Sharon and Gavish moved up to within good seeing distance of the Egyptian front. At 2245 the division commander ordered all his artillery to open fire. In twenty minutes the batteries got off seven thousand rounds; the reverberations from the dunes were deafening. As the barrage ceased on signal, the infantry—two thousand men—swept down from the dunes, spread out so that at least one battalion could hit each trench line from the flank. From where Sharon's artillery stood, two searchlights were beamed on the scene, throwing the positions into clear relief. The hand-to-hand fight lasted an hour, the Israelis going at the trenches from the embankments, throwing grenades and firing Uzis. By midnight they had cleared the first two miles of Umm Gataf southward as far as the line of ridges.

The paratroop battalion, landing atop the dunes without incident, was now fighting all-out at the artillery base, burning supply, turning the guns, mopping up crews, and capturing prisoners.

The northern task force, having won its fight on the El Arish road, had swung southeast and was attacking Umm Gataf from the rear. This was at about 0100 on 6 June.

At 0130 the engineers came up to clear the mines from the highway and open a lane for the armor. The first four tanks clanked through. The fifth tank rolled onto a live mine, blew a track, and blocked the road. The engineers started again, clearing a lane along a second line and using a flail to do it. By 0230 the work was complete, and the armor began feeding through.

None of this relieved Sharon's worries. Although he soon had two battalions of armor inside the enemy position, he knew that the Egyptians had at least sixty tanks still under crews and fit to move and fire. He wanted to keep the battle zone clear, so he ordered the paratroops (they had finished their work) to withdraw north to the dunes with their dead and wounded. It was well timed: the melee between the two armored forces began immediately afterward. Throughout, it was wildly confused—a continuing fire exchange at anywhere from ten to fifty meters. Some of the M-54's got mixed up with the Israeli Shermans and began firing at their own people. Tuesday's dawn came at 0400, and with the growing light, the Egyptians seemed to sense acutely the desperation of their position and lashed out harder than ever. It was all over within thirty minutes: daylight had worked in favor of the side with the expert marksmen.

At 0200 Gavish had asked Sharon the question: "When shall I put Yoffe's second brigade through?" (Yoffe's train was following after the brigade.) Sharon replied: "Have them follow close behind my tanks; in two hours they should be able to break through." The column came on at 0415; the guess had not been too accurate. Sharon had his tanks move to the south of the highway to give the brigade free way. The column buzzed right on through a live battlefield without losing a man or a vehicle. By 0600 the brigade was through Abu Agueila and heading west, and Sharon was himself quitting Umm Gataf to go to the village.

Gavish too went west behind the brigade in his motorized command post. For three hours he was out of communication because the radios would not cut through, and this tried him sorely—especially when General Rabin had to fly to him to learn what was happening.

Sharon had lost forty men killed and one hundred twenty wounded, while destroying sixty tanks, one hundred ten guns, sixty mortars, and many half-tracks. About one thousand Egyptians died defending the sand hills of Umm Gataf.

There was no pause after battle, however. The force sent to block against Queisima had folded back into the main body without seeing the village, with no time to visit, one league away, the great artesian spring of Ein-Qudeirat, the Kadesh Barnea of Biblical times, where Moses' people stayed thirty-eight years. Sharon's vanguard had already hit the road out of Abu Agueila by 0600, although his command post lingered there for some hours.

Where the road from Bir Hasne crosses the Queisima-Nakhl road, his division front had its next fight in midmorning, colliding with part of the enemy garrison that was beating westward from Queisima. Not much came of it: hit a glancing blow that shattered some of their chariots, the Egyptians fired a few Parthian rounds for the sake of honor and fled into the desert.

The route of movement had been dictated by Gavish. Once again the army commander, who was all over the battlefield, had altered his plans in order to shorten the war. When he met Sharon near Jebel Hilal, Gavish was no longer worrying about the northern axis; he knew that Tal had won his right-of-way on the first day. The problem now was to crush the Egyptians before they could get away. Sharon wanted to take the open road to Bir Hasne because it would tax the division less. Gavish said: "You will go straight cross-country to Nakhl." He hoped to bag Shazali's forces and parts of the Egyptian 6th Division.

The direct line to Nakhl, as a raven would fly, is not even a respectable wadi. There is no trace. Washboarded as by a giant hand, the ditches and potholes between the ribs of this stretch of desert are deep enough to lose a jeep from sight. Only walking it would be worse than trying to follow along on wheels and tracks. Division Sharon bumped along, laboring, sweating, manhandling vehicles out of trouble, wearing itself to near-exhaustion, and at last foundering, largely because it ran out of fuel. There had to be a supply drop. This tortured movement, the hardest grind given any division, took two and one-half days.

Still short of Nakhl, Sharon got word from higher command that an Egyptian mechanized brigade was at Themed and heading west on the run. This happened on the fourth day. Nothing more was needed to quicken the pace of Sharon's tired troops. Gavish also told him: "The independent brigade is in pursuit and I am putting it under your command." This is the same brigade that had been harassing and holding the Egyptians based on Kuntilla. Sending a message to the brigade: "Just keep coming fast," Sharon put his G-3 (operations officer) aloft in a Bell helicopter to look for the enemy column. His foremost tanks had just begun to roll into Nakhl when a few minutes later the message came through from the observer aloft: "They're within five miles of Nakhl and coming straight at you." It was hardly needed. Looking east, Sharon could see a dust column high in the sky.

With not a minute to lose, he set up a division-size ambush rigged around the road intersection inside Nakhl, with one armored infantry battalion and one tank on each prong, extending to the east and south. They would beat out the game by surprise fire from the flanks, thus driving it into the killing fire within the village. At the same time Sharon sent a message to the com-

Breaks, while rare during the Israeli offensive, were remarkably relaxed.
Clockwise from above: picture-taking on a road in Syria; praying; eating an
orange in a tank turret; reading mail from home at Gaza; studying a captured Syrian propaganda booklet; and the inevitable potato-peeling.

mander of the independent brigade: "When we stop them, you come on and hit them from the rear."

Sharon then passed along a word of caution to all units: "Nobody shoots until they are well within the trap." His own forces were hidden behind low hills. The front of the Egyptian column was within three hundred meters of Nakhl, and well past the two battalions that had been sent out to the flanks, when Sharon gave the order to fire. There was a blast from every cannon and infantry weapon that could be brought to bear. Ten tanks were set afire with the first salvo. The killing and destruction (it was hardly a fight) went on for two hours. The Egyptian column was strung out twenty miles to the east, far beyond reach of the division's weapons. But the independent brigade quickly closed on the Egyptian rear.

One thousand meters to the east, eight Egyptian Centurions, hull down behind the banks of a shallow ravine, continued to shell Nakhl, and men were getting hit. One extension of the ambush, roughly parallel to it, had a clear view of this target. Sharon asked the brigade commander to engage the Egyptians; he hesitated, having only one Centurion with him. Right then four Mysteres came over. Sharon sent them against the eight Centurions, and all were destroyed by bombs. Mysteres and Mirages began to appear in formations of four. Sharon directed them in successive strikes eastward against the Egyptian column.

From Nakhl the conflagration and carnage wrought by bombs, cannon, and napalm stretched eastward almost as far as Themed. Death Valley, the troops were soon calling it. Within Nakhl village the din was terrible. Added to the roar of the guns, flights of choppers were coming in with fuel and water and flying out with the wounded and the few dead. Just before sundown on Thursday, 8 June, the fighting ended. No more fire came from the east. Many of the Egyptians fled on foot to the desert. There was no attempt to pursue. When it was over and twilight came, Sharon thought to check the temperature. It was 110 degrees.

As the division moved on toward Mitla Pass, orders came that it should prepare for a march to Sharm-el-Sheikh. At 0300 a message on radio canceled that out. Sharon was so tired that when a staff officer awakened him to tell him the thing had been scrubbed and he could rest easy, he could not even murmur a protest.

More usable loot fell into Israel's hands out of the Nakhl action than from any other fight in Sinai. Among the prizes were sixty tanks, as many half-tracks, two hundred trucks, and enough guns to serve several battalions.

An aerial survey showed the figures. Of the 536 tanks that the Egyptians had left strewn across Sinai, not counting the full park of vehicles that one brigade had left neatly aligned under camouflage netting at Kauraya, a base not far from Kuntilla, less than one hundred would ever again be serviceable.

All others were debris added to the desert waste. Possibly it was the sight of this that inspired General Yoffe, on his first day back in civilian clothes as national parks director, to start a new campaign. The paper read: "Let us quit littering the countryside. We must keep all things beautiful."

Ten thousand Egyptians were captured in Sinai. The estimate is that fifteen thousand were killed in battle, although Cairo puts the number at seven thousand. Either way, no more than two thirds of the Arab soldiery deployed into Sinai must have made it back to Suez.

Brigadier General Avraham Yoffe's men were as mad as hornets and "ready to eat stones." He could feel it so the morning he jumped off with his first brigade from the old Nabatean town of Ruhaiba, marked now only by ruins. The time was 0815 on 5 June when they hit the road.

Yoffe, as wise as a treeful of owls about nature, human and otherwise, one of Israel's favorite citizens and well known in the United States, knew why his men were so surly. The prolonged defensive wait had over-charged them. That weekend some of them had gone home, and their families had aired doubts that the army could still win. Too much time had been lost.

The outfit was not more unusual than its leader. Here was the light division of the Sinai invasion, formed of only two armored brigades with supporting artillery and the essential attachments of engineers and signal and service units. All were reservists called up on 19 May. Only one brigade was going with Yoffe for the time being. The cross-country route to the west, through a wadi, skirting the dunes, would not sustain the full division column. The second brigade would follow the better road where Division Sharon was to break through and join Yoffe somewhere around Jebel Libni.

Like his command, Yoffe must have been an eleventh-hour improvisation. At age fifty-four, two years retired from the army, knowing the land and its lore as few other Sabras do, he was serving as director of Israel's national park system. When, on 23 May, he was summoned to General Gavish's headquarters at Beersheba, he went wearing sports togs, thinking his counsel would be sought for an hour or so. Told that he was to get into uniform and why, he did not raise a hair, although he had never before commanded armor or led a division in war.

From the beginning, Yoffe understood his role and was content with it. Light as it was, the division would play the dustpan in the classic maneuver through which armor, operating pretty much on its own, fragments an enemy force and sweeps it rearward. (The operation of the late General Wavell at Sidi Barrani in North Africa is a prime example from World War II.) While protecting General Tal's flank to the north and driving south to strike the enemy's rear, Yoffe's first brigade would try to avoid open battle. Less content with that role was Yoffe's Chief of Staff and protégé, forty-year-old Colonel "Bren" Adan, a pint-size soldier, head of the armored school, who loves a head-on fight.

Brigadier General Avraham Yoffe

The brigade and division headquarters rolled and bumped on through the morning without incident—the Centurions forward, with reconnaissance elements breaking the trail. Halfway back in the column, Yoffe rode in a half-track next to that of the brigade commander. All the way he had excellent communications with Division Sharon some miles to his left and Division Tal on his right. The army was equipped with the PRC series of field radios, like those the U.S. Army uses in Vietnam. In late afternoon the column front reached its first objective, the road juncture south of Bir Lafham, fifty miles from its departure line. Yoffe knew by then that Tal had all but won his first battle and that Sharon was forming up more promptly than he had hoped for the most crucial encounter of all at Umm Gataf.

Yet while Israel's armor was moving at breakneck speed on all fronts, the fortunes of war were strangely perverse. Not only was schedule everywhere maintained; on all three main axes through Sinai, the timetable was actually being beaten. The penetrations went faster than planned. This

caused such disarrangement that the burden of the fight could not be evenly distributed; and a grotesquely disproportionate share fell to some units.

Most of all this was true in Yoffe's division despite all that the big man could do to control it. Unkind fate and the friction of the battlefield had determined that, from start to finish—although there were two armored brigades moving ever deeper into enemy country—most of the hard fighting would be done by one brigade. Out of that brigade, one battalion was ever in the van, bearing the brunt.

Yoffe's first brigade was commanded by Colonel Ishahar (Iska) Shadmi, a fifty-year-old civilian soldier, manager of the skyscraping Shalom Mayer Tower, the most conspicuous landmark in downtown Tel Aviv. Iska is a highly congenial man, who in the field couples a keen eye for ground with the nerve for instant decision. His brigade was first over the border at 0815, pointing for the primary objective: the main road just below Bir Lafham. It was thirty-six miles to the west, over untamed desert, unmarked by trail.

Seven miles short of Bir Lafham at 1400, his first battalion, under Lieutenant Colonel Avraham Bar-Am, a twenty-eight-year-old regular, fought its first engagement. An Egyptian antitank company with ten guns in position barred the way. Bar-Am moved to the high ground off their flank and in a thirty-minute fight destroyed the unit. But he also temporarily lost four Centurions, which became beached by the soft sand of the upper dunes. Shadmi moved right on, leaving the four tanks and their crews behind. He figured they would be freed by the recovery vehicles coming along in the division train and would catch up later. (They did, at Jebel Libni.)

Bar-Am's forward elements got to the main road at 1600 hours on Monday. The Egyptians in the Bir Lafham hedgehog a thousand meters to the northwest were instantly aware of the arrival. Shadmi's orders were "to clear the road with fire." His column front was already under fire from the tanks, artillery, and antitank guns northward as Bar-Am moved to deploy, facing south. Since it looked like much too hot a corner, Shadmi asked permission

Retreating on Sinai, the Egyptians abandoned military hardware— most of it Russian-made—worth well over a billion dollars. The Israelis found the deserted surface- to-air (SAM) missile base above virtually intact; even the complex radar guidance equipment had been left in operational order.

to pull in his horns a bit. Back came the order from higher command: "You must hold on the road." The Egyptian artillery, based less than two miles away, had the movement clearly in sight and was already ranging on the road. Promptly Bar-Am lost to fire from an antitank gun one Centurion and one company commander, who was standing in his turret.

Colonel Adan arrived about then, with an unusual request. In both 1948 and 1956 he had captured Abu Agueila, and that hot spot was very much on his mind. He said to Shadmi: "Give me your other battalion of armor. I'll get the battalion of Arik's [Sharon] that is coming along north of the dunes and have a go at it." This, decidedly, was not according to plan.

Then Adan added most casually: "By the way, I have information that two enemy brigades are coming at you from Jebel Libni." With a vision of being trapped between fires, Shadmi protested: "Then you must leave both battalions with me." Adan replied: "Good-by. You won't need both battalions. Egyptians can't fight at night. You will take care of them." Too soon he was gone south, taking the second battalion.

At 2200, one hour after dark, Shadmi saw a long line of dimout lights winking on the road from the south. It was the enemy column, approaching not to attack him but to reinforce El Arish. He had sent forth two hours earlier a reconnaissance party in three jeeps to monitor movement from that direction. Now two miles off and abreast of the enemy force, the party radioed him: "At least one reinforced armored brigade is moving on you." Shadmi wanted to put out mines but did not have time. So he advanced just one of Bar-Am's companies to form a block on the main road. He knew that, from his command post, placed on high ground about one and one-half miles to the east of the road, he could not get a line on armor moving in the dark. But from the low ground along the road, the men at the block would get the oncoming armor in silhouette. By then Shadmi no longer worried about the fire coming at his rear from Bir Lafham. The other guns had quit at dark and the artillery, though continuing, was highly erratic.

Because of the dropouts stranded along the dunes to the east, the one company mustered only nine Centurions for the block. The Egyptian brigade came right on in column, obviously unwarned of Shadmi's presence by any message from Bir Lafham. The engagement opened at one thousand meters, and by rare luck and good shooting, the first salvo from the block hit and exploded seven light-skinned vehicles and one M-55 tank. Where all had been darkness, Shadmi now had a fully illuminated battlefield.

Surprised and shocked, the Egyptian armor at first recoiled. Then, after firing briefly from column, the tanks deployed on a broad front on both sides of the road and advanced to the El Arish Wadi. This dry wash, where the confrontation occurred, is flat-bedded and not too boulder-strewn, about one thousand meters wide. No real tank obstacle, the wadi still hexed and held the Egyptian tanks once they entered upon it.

Thirty-five of them took position in line within the wadi. The fight became a gun duel at a distance of nine hundred to twelve hundred meters, an ideal range for the crews in the Centurions, although soon the volume of fire from the wadi became too heavy for the nine tanks. Shadmi had then gone back toward his position on the high ground. At 0100 on 6 June, several battalions of artillery that had moved up to support the attack across the wadi barraged Shadmi's general front. The guns to the north continued to

The booty they collected on Sinai was probably an unexpected surprise to the advancing Israelis, for the Egyptians failed to destroy what they could not remove. Moreover, many of the surface-to-air missiles that the Israelis found were in firing position (opposite page, top), although few had gotten off the ground. Another discovery was the peculiar instruction plaque on a missile launching device (left). Operational instructions were given in Russian and English, but not in Arabic.

hammer away. It was careless, wild shooting by excited men and not too terrible to bear. Shadmi's own guns—from the tanks and the self-propelled 105's—disregarded this nuisance from north and south and concentrated fire on the wadi. He thought he was making money, but he could not be sure.

Far to the southeast, Colonel Adan heard the roar and saw the flashes, had second thoughts about the go at Abu Agueila, and sent the second battalion back. But it had wasted four hours of fuel, which proved costly.

Shadmi held the battalion back, intending at first light (about 0400) to try an outflanking move eastward of the enemy tanks in the wadi. Dawn came, and with it came a thick ground mist. As the mist slowly lifted, Shadmi saw on a high dune, one and one-half miles directly south of the wadi, another twenty-three tanks, all M-54's and M-55's. That changed his mind about the maneuver; it would have invited sudden death. Then, glancing at the wadi, he saw seventeen of the Egyptian tanks burning, and he said to Bar-Am: "That's half of them; we're doing all right where we are."

By 0700 on Tuesday, Bar-Am knew his battalion was through for a time. He called Shadmi to say: "We'd keep on but we're out of ammunition." Essential resupplies had not yet arrived to refuel the well-traveled second battalion for the long pull. Shadmi took one of its companies and placed it behind the first battalion to continue the fire fight while Bar-Am's outfit was withdrawn platoon by platoon to a spot two miles to the east to rearm and refuel. Because of the belated arrival of supplies, Bar-Am and his battalion were on that spot until 1100. Two hours earlier the Egyptians, having fought through the night, had disengaged and gone south, depriving the second battalion of any real share in the fight. There were now twenty-four tanks ablaze in the wadi. Shadmi had lost one tank burned and one temporarily disabled.

At 1100 Shadmi got orders from Yoffe to move out. The first battalion was ready. But the second's fuel tanks were still nearly empty. By this circumstance, the worn battalion again got the call. Bar-Am's tanks took off cross-country, through the blazing armor in the wadi, without pausing to look back. Simultaneously Shadmi heard behind him the roar and clamor of General Tal's attack on the Bir Lafham hedgehog. His headquarters—three half-tracks and two jeeps—was already moving toward the road intersection south of Bir Lafham. As they reached the intersection, a soldier sitting next to Shadmi pulled at his sleeve and gestured frantically to the north, his teeth chattering so that he could not speak. Shadmi looked. Coming at him, in full flight from Bir Lafham, less than one-half mile away, were two Egyptian T-54 tanks, three armored personnel carriers, and four infantry-loaded lorries. The second battalion had moved east to refuel. Shadmi called Bar-Am, saying: "I need help." In two minutes, the first battalion's tanks had turned about. Firing over Shadmi's head, two of the Centurions, using two rounds apiece, demolished the two T-54's, at a range of fifteen hundred meters. The command post group took on the rest of the Egyptians with small arms and the 105 recoilless; the Arabs reacted to the fire by leaping from the vehicles in panic flight into the dunes.

Shadmi had asked for an air strike in the early morning against what was left of the Egyptian brigade strung out along the road to Jebel Libni. Strafing the column, Israeli planes had not only wiped out most of the guns of two artillery battalions, but they had also flushed the Egyptians from the tanks and vehicles to seek nearby ground cover. By the time Bar-Am moved

Some of the fiercest fighting on the Sinai occurred at the Mitla Pass, directly east of Suez. Involving hundreds of tanks, the battle lasted an entire night and resulted in the almost complete destruction of Egyptian equipment along the sixteen-mile-long pass. Most of the hardware shown above was demolished by Israeli fighter bombers.

OVERLEAF: *An aerial view of the wreckage-strewn road through Mitla Pass.*

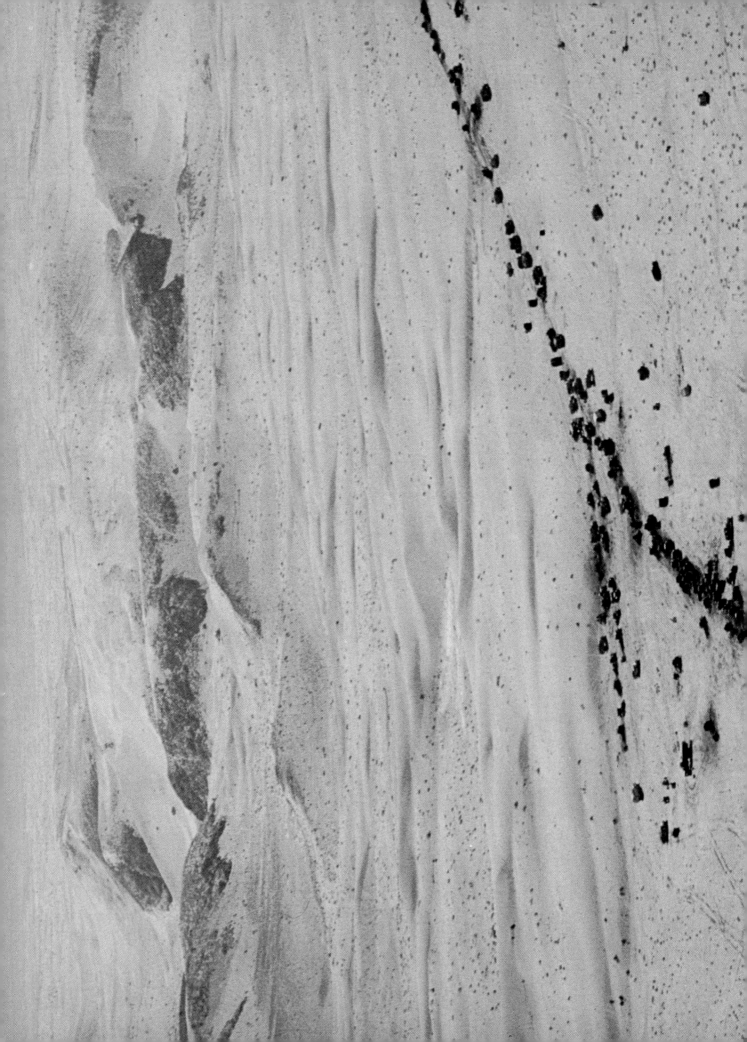

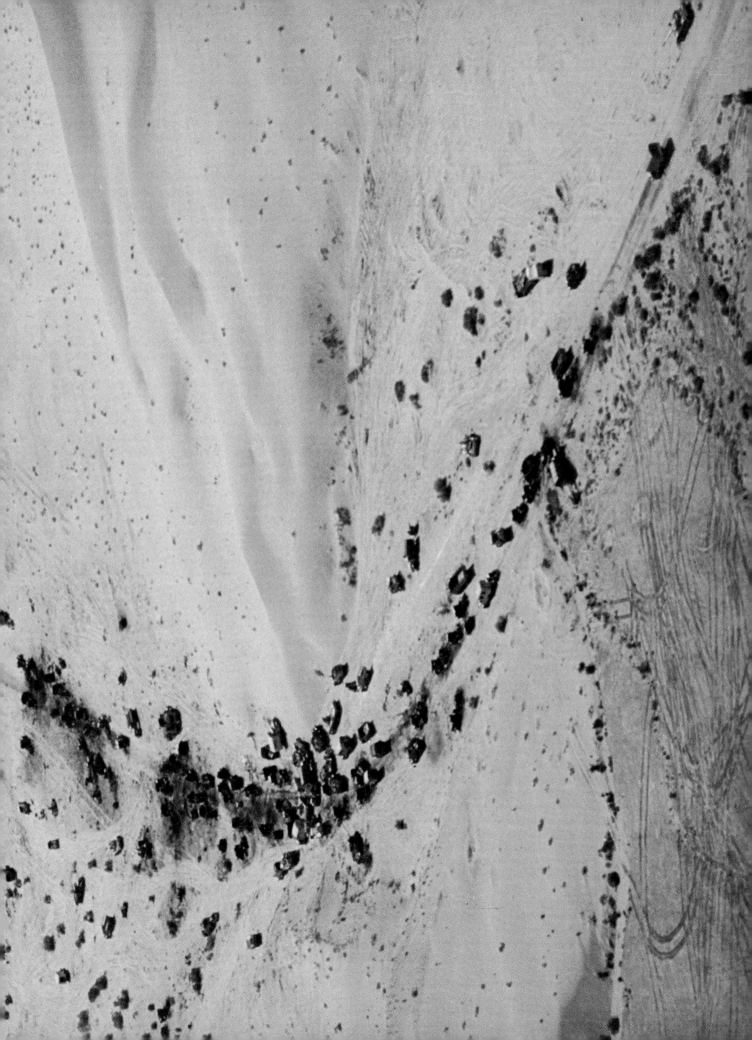

through, with Shadmi's group following, they were under armor again and resisting. There was fighting of sorts all the way to Jebel Libni, twenty miles distant, with luckless Egyptian crews working their tanks and antitank guns singly when all semblance of command control had vanished. That day Shadmi saw the enemy change from a seemingly organized force to a bewildered army striving vainly to recover—not yet a panic-stricken mob.

Coming first to the enemy camp five miles north of Jebel Libni and finding it impossibly strong in armor, antitank guns, and men, Bar-Am said on radio to Shadmi: "I'm sorry, this time it's just asking too much." It was a modest demurrer from a fighter who still did not know the outer limit of his own resources. Shadmi replied: "Keep contact and don't go charging in." Bar-Am waited, two thousand meters short of the entrenched camp. The command vehicles rolled on south, Shadmi knowing that another fight was coming and that he would need his second battalion, which was following.

Through the night, Yoffe, though forward with the brigade, had let Shadmi run his own fight, and correctly so. Yoffe had his own set of problems—dealing with the second brigade which in early morning had passed through Sharon's division at Umm Gataf; forestalling collision with any of Tal's units if they drove south earlier than expected; and above all, assuring the forwarding of supplies to the division front. Yoffe would have been better off in a helicopter, but there was none to spare. Ammunition and fuel were being spent faster than was expected. All water for the troops had to come over the roads and tracks. Even in Sinai, where temperatures run to 120 degrees, Israel's soldiers do not take salt tablets for protection against heat. Water, water, in unending flow, brought forward in milk trucks, is their therapy. Shadmi's troops had taken off from Ruhaiba with only one meal and had been without food since. Yoffe himself ate nothing during the first three days but a half-dozen oranges.

Just before noon on Tuesday, when Shadmi had turned south to catch up with the first battalion, he and Yoffe parted company. With enough of Shadmi's tanks left behind to defend his command group, Yoffe held fast at the crossroads. He knew that one of Tal's spearheads, after breaking through the Bir Lafham hedgehog, would soon come up, and he hoped to coordinate Tal's further movement south with that of his own forces. Some minutes after Shadmi slipped away, Tal's first tank arrived. Standing in the turret was Yoffe's nephew, Captain Amir. There was no time for talk. The brigade commander was right behind him. Yoffe said to him: "Hold where you are! Let all of my vehicles move out before you regroup or do anything."

With that, Yoffe was up and gone, driving for Jebel Libni and arriving there just in time to see Shadmi stage his next fight. Again, he let Shadmi manage the battle. The general was now sweating double. If there should develop a main tank battle along the line he was now moving, with the Egyptian 4th Armored counterattacking from around Bir Gifgafa and the Wadi Meliez, he would need every fighting vehicle under his command. However, his second brigade, having arrived at noon of 6 June just east of the Jebel (the mountain from which the village and camp at Jebel Libni get their name), had first run into resistance from antitank guns and artillery and then run out of gas. So it sat there quite uselessly a few miles away amid an exchange of fires that hurt nothing very much. Division Yoffe, for the second day, remained a brigade. Some of Shadmi's vehicles had refueled from an air drop.

Colonel Bren Adan

Shadmi and his brigade launched their attack on the entrenched camp at Jebel Libni at 1600 on 6 June, after waiting until the second battalion of tanks had come on from Bir Lafham. It was not a good situation. The Egyptians in observation posts could see everything he did.

He deployed his second battalion on the right, the tired first battalion on the left, each being spread over a front of about twenty-five hundred meters. There was a white hut in the center of the camp; he made this the limiting point between battalions. Otherwise, he could not see what the camp contained, such was the dust cloud raised by armor churning about. Forward of it, however, within about six hundred meters of his line, was an earth wall slotted with about fifty bunkers to protect the Egyptian tanks firing in his direction. The spread of the bunkers was wide enough to checkmate all of the first battalion and part of the second, which was on the lower ground. To Shadmi's amazement, the enemy deployed only eighteen tanks, out of more than fifty present, and put them all in the first eighteen slots opposite the first battalion's extreme left flank, instead of distributing them evenly along the whole bunker line.

Thereupon Colonel Bar-Am of the first battalion began shifting his tanks to the left to get them on a spur of the Jebel. The Egyptian armor made no attempt to interfere. The second battalion's commander had quite different worries. Shadmi kept hearing from him: "All I see is dust. I am eating dust. I keep firing into the dust. And I hear from the first battalion, 'Take care; they are moving around your flank.'" Some of the Egyptian armor was slipping west through the dust, but it stayed invisible. There was much blind firing. Shadmi's second battalion lost two tanks and two half-tracks.

From the spur on the Jebel where Bar-Am's left had moved up, one tank captain drove forward to get on the flank of the eighteen Egyptian 34's, 54's, and 55's. A second tank followed him, had its engine stall, and fell out. The captain, however, found the spot he sought, opened fire, and killed the six tanks nearest him. The first battalion destroyed the other twelve tanks firing from the front. The fire fight was over in two minutes. Later twenty to thirty shell casings were found beside each of the ruined Egyptian tanks. They had tried; there were twenty-two fresh hits on Bar-Am's tanks, but none had been knocked out. Despite its feeling of futility because of the dust storm, the second battalion had killed eleven Arab tanks with its fire. The rest of the Egyptian armor slid away to the west, although artillery shelling of the brigade's position went on until 2200.

General Tal arrived soon after dark. The brigade that had slashed through Bir Lafham was following him south and would turn west, trying for Suez on another axis. General Gavish also flew in by helicopter. He was alternately commanding the field army from two motorized command posts— one that had moved behind Tal into El Arish, the other that had followed Yoffe into Jebel Libni. Double-staffed, the command posts moved in five armored personnel carriers; the chopper afforded Gavish a shuttle. Most of the first day he had spent on Tal's front, where the problem was explosive, and the situation rapidly changing. That evening he had flown to Sharon's division, for the attack on Umm Gataf was the largest and most decisive undertaking of the campaign.

Gavish, like the others, had slept only in winks. It seemed not to show. At the age of forty-one, Gavish is tall, angular, with a bronzed, hawklike

Colonel Ishahar Shadmi

OVERLEAF: *Egyptian MIG's, two of the few that were still in the air on the fifth day of the war, strafe an Israeli convoy on its way to the Suez Canal. Note the Israeli soldiers (bottom) diving for cover.*

After defeating the Egyptians at the battle of Mitla Pass, the Israeli forces advanced the rest of the way to the Suez Canal against lighter resistance. The Israeli soldier above, nearing a Suez bridge, was a strafing victim of the Egyptians' last-ditch defense of the waterway. Below, an Israeli prepares to taste the fruits of victory. The ship on the opposite page was sunk near Ismailia to block traffic in the canal, by then partly controlled by Israel.

face. One of the original brain-trusters of Israel's army, he had not held a field command in fifteen years. Looking imperious and domineering, he is the Quiet Man, deeply reflective, and so self-controlled that when directing a battle, he sounds as if he were conducting a field exercise.

By Tuesday night he had decided, to his own relief, that the Egyptian armor of the second line would not counterattack in strength. In consequence, he would not keep divisions Tal and Yoffe together, holding around Bir Tamada, but would continue attacking, accepting increased risks by driving for the Gidy and Mitla passes simultaneously. It was his intention to stay at Jebel Libni for two days while the campaign was pushed to conclusion.

Gavish's conference with his two division commanders was held at 0200 on Wednesday, 7 June, near the Jebel Libni airdrome. By then, the three men had been going for forty-two hours, taking such rest as they could find in moving vehicles. Orders had been oral. The two division columns would move parallel for a time—Yoffe's on the main road to Bir Hasne, Tal's over the rough desert west of it, later turning right to head for Bir Gifgafa. The other brigade being still stranded to the east, Shadmi was given his piece of the general movement: he would move on Bir Hasne as quickly as possible.

Yoffe took him aside and said: "Do me a little favor; send a combat force east to ease the pressure on second brigade." Shadmi peeled off one

battalion to take care of that task. The first battalion of the first brigade was fueled, armed, and ready to go at first light on Wednesday, around 0400. The brigade still stood as a box, the way it had bivouacked, artillery forming one side, the three attack battalions forming the other three. As the box began to dissolve, so that the main column could march south while the one battalion went east, something happened. Six miles to the east, Yoffe's second brigade had gotten a few vehicles moving and had routed the Egyptians from their blockade. About fifteen of the fleeing enemy vehicles came charging straight in toward one corner of Shadmi's block. Fire poured on them from three sides. With visions of his men dying from their own bullets amid the confusion, Shadmi yelled: "Cease fire! Cease fire!" But no one heeded. The wild melee lasted five minutes and ended when the surviving Egyptians jumped from their tanks and trucks and fled into the desert.

The second brigade arrived, its fuel and ammunition spent. Yoffe relieved his feelings by relieving the commander. Again, Shadmi had to shove off, fronting for the division. Following orders, his one battalion moved east to wipe out what was left of the enemy force that had engaged the second brigade.

Having left his armored infantry battalion to tie down the Jebel Libni area, Shadmi used Bar-Am's battalion of Centurions and two battalions of artillery to capture Bir Hasne, which showed on the map as a fortified camp, at 1100 on 7 June. In so doing, he knocked out five more Egyptian tanks. One T-34 directly charged his half-track; the artillery saved him, killing the tank at three hundred meters range with two 105 rounds. Thereafter his problem at Bir Hasne lay in coping with prisoners. They came by the hundreds, with hands up but still carrying their rifles. That danger was accepted. By noon the number was several thousand. They were shooed into an administration building, and two squads in half-tracks were left to guard it.

To Bar-Am, Shadmi said: "You keep on going south." It was easier said than done. From that point on, the Egyptians had sewn the highway and its shoulders with mines—thousands of them. The sight scared the Israelis silly until one tank, backing away, ran over two mines and squashed them flat. The Egyptians had neglected to arm all but one in twenty or so of their mines. Still, they had to thread their way carefully, testing each mine to determine the hot from the cold. Gingerly, Bar-Am moved on, his riflemen kicking the mines aside. At 1500 he reached Bir Tamada; it had taken his battalion three hours to go the three and one-half miles from Bir Hasne, since there were mines all the way. En route his armor had engaged—and destroyed—twelve T-34's and T-54's, but they had passed far more burned-out enemy armor than that (fifty-one tanks altogether). The air strikes had taken a heavy toll.

Midway between Bir Hasne and Bir Tamada, Shadmi observed great columns of dust blotting out the sky about twenty miles to the east. He thought at first a sandstorm was sweeping toward him, then concluded it could not be so because the curtain looked too irregular and came on too slowly. It had to be columns of vehicles. He was already in the Wadi Meliez, the base of the Egyptian 4th Armored Division. He had no notion of how much of the 4th was left; he did know that with less than two battalions present, he was unsupported on left and right.

There were now only nine tanks with him, and looking at them, he concluded his force was so insignificant that he had nothing to lose. He spread

Still treading an ocean of sand eight days after their battle had been lost, three Egyptian stragglers make for Kantara. The photograph was taken from a helicopter flying over the Sinai desert wastes on June 15.

them out to the east of Bir Tamada in the direction from which the dust curtain was moving. Soon he could see hundreds of vehicles moving over the desert; then it occurred to him that most of his own tanks must be nearly dry. Scouting about, he found drums of aviation fuel at the Bir Tamada air base, but no gas-carrying vehicle. Pushing the search, he found a tanker that the Egyptians had tried to wreck with explosives. One of his boys said: "Don't worry, Iska, we'll have it going for you in another hour." It was then about 1515.

Colonel Adan, the Chief of Staff, arrived and quickly briefed Shadmi on General Sharon's advance toward Nakhl and on the efforts of Shazali's forces to break through or go around the independent brigade there. He said to Shadmi: "You must go hell-bent for the entrance to the Mitla."

Shadmi stayed on at the Bir Tamada crossroads, with four fuelless tanks. Bar-Am by then had twelve, three more having overtaken the column. But a few minutes later, when he started out alone for Parker's Memorial, a landmark fifteen miles east of Mitla Pass, only five tanks were running under their own power; four, out of gas, were being towed. As Bar-Am headed south, the Egyptians stirring the dust cloud changed course and headed toward Shadmi at the crossroads. With his tanks run dry and hundreds of enemy tanks coming at him, he had a sunk feeling expressed in words that he dared not say aloud: "I've lost my battle."

But it was not quite hopeless. Shadmi rounded up three jericans of gas and personally ran about to all his foundered vehicles, putting a little gas in each tank. When he had finished this labor, the Egyptians were not more than a thousand meters away. Right then he got a call from his second battalion commander on the radio: "We're almost there." Shadmi replied: "You come up fast and save this unit. But start firing." The second battalion turned on the power and the guns. Its first salvos wiped out more than one hundred of the enemy vehicles, and with their destruction, most of the enemy movement was shunted south toward Mitla Pass. This happened at about 1830. When darkness fell a half-hour later, other vehicles singly or in twos and threes pressed in against Shadmi and the reconnaissance tanks at the crossroad. It became difficult to distinguish friend from foe in the continuing exchange of fire at less than forty meters. One sergeant got tired of it, placed himself to the fore with a 105 recoilless rifle, and knocked off the last thirteen Egyptian carriers to enter the block. Shadmi kept two companies of the second battalion at Bir Tamada and sent a third to support Bar-Am at Parker's Memorial. It was needed.

With only nine Centurions left, four of them being towed, Bar-Am had embarked on about as desperate a mission as could be given a tanker. He was to march across the front of an army in full retreat, block the escape hatch toward which it was funneling, and try to hold on, with no real hope that help would come. Long before this forlorn party reached Parker's Memorial, Egyptian tanks—T-34's, Stalins, and T-54's—were moving along on both sides of them, ahead of them, and to the rear. They were so close that Bar-Am could have hit them with bird shot. In the dark they could not see his markings. All that saved him was that, seeing tanks under tow, they mistook him for their own, just another parcel of fugitives. He kept silent; so did they; so did the 105 battery that had come along. Shadmi prodded him on the radio: "Push on! Push on!" Finally Bar-Am bridled, replying: "Push,

Beaten to Sharm-el-Sheikh by a naval force that moved down the Gulf of Aqaba, disappointed paratroopers had to forego a combat drop for an uneventful landing on the airstrip at the tip of the Sinai Peninsula (opposite, above). Israel's bloodless take-over of Sharm-el-Sheikh lifted Nasser's blockade of the Strait of Tiran, an immediate provocation of the war. Below right, an Israeli plants his nation's flag on shore as his comrades unload supplies from a boat.

how can I push? They have me four ways. I can't stop and I can't go faster."

By the time Bar-Am reached Parker's Memorial, Shadmi's brigade was strung out over one hundred miles of desert, from the east end of Mitla Pass to Bir Lafham. Bar-Am announced his arrival to Shadmi in these words: "I'm here. It's no place. I can be hit from any direction." Shadmi replied: "Then find a better spot and God bless you." He did not expect to see Bar-Am again.

Bar-Am, still towing, moved right on into the Pass itself, amid a welter of Egyptian tanks, antitank and antiaircraft guns, armored personnel carriers, trucks, and jeeps, all converging toward the one large hole in the mountain wall. The struggle thickened. Hod's planes had been cannonading and bombing Egyptian traffic, starting at the extreme western end of the eighteen-mile-long defile, since early that morning. Block rapidly piled on block, and the choke now extended eastward over two thirds of the Pass in a sinuous, blazing, and exploding barrier of blasted machinery, melting metal, and piled-up ashes—a most melancholy graveyard of a doomed army.

Finding a flat-topped knob just off the paved highway, Bar-Am there formed a Custer ring of the nine tanks, enclosing the battery of 105's, so that he would have fire in all directions. It took the Egyptians some minutes to understand what was happening. Then they reacted. The laager, or defensive circle, was shelled from short range by a body of tanks, after which twenty-two of them (mainly M-54's) came charging on, some heading directly toward Bar-Am's position, others swinging wide in an attempt to escape via the road. Shadmi got a message from Bar-Am: "I think this is the end." One of his sergeants, a tank commander on the rear of the formation, saw two tanks turn toward the Pass just off his flank, mistakenly thought his own formation was moving west, and followed the pair for a mile. Then he got a clear view of them in silhouette, recognized them as Stalins, and gunned and destroyed them from behind at a range of thirty meters. His work done, the sergeant turned about. At the laager, Bar-Am had done as well. The twenty other Egyptian tanks lay dead, their hulls ablaze, at various distances outside the perimeter. Soon after midnight Bar-Am called Shadmi again: "I finished them." The few armored infantrymen with Bar-Am supported the tanks from fire positions away from the road, using only machine guns.

The moon came late Wednesday night, and there was no real need of it. This was not a darkened battlefield. At Shadmi's position, as at Bar-Am's, the desert and the sub-ridges shone bright from the glare of burning tanks and transports, the illumination extending as far as the eye could see. Motorized remnants continued to appear in the lighted areas at both positions, most of them moving in thin-skinned carriers during the hours of early morning. There was no trouble sighting; nothing impaired the shooting but fatigue and the choking dust. Panicked, bent only on flight, the Egyptians made no further attempt to destroy either party. A few of the lesser vehicles, mostly half-tracks, made good their escape to the west by using side trails, unknown to the Israelis. But not one tank got through.

By 0800 Thursday morning, most of the pressure was off, and it was well so. Bar-Am's soldiers were dead beat. Gunners were falling asleep after loading, pitching forward onto their guns. A crew chief would pick one up, shake him, and ask: "Why don't you fire?" Staring, the gunner would ask: "Fire at what?" Not a tank had been lost, although one Centurion bore the scars of

Limping into Malta six days after being attacked in the eastern Mediterranean by Israeli planes and boats, the U.S.S. Liberty *shows the scars of a mysterious assault made on her. On June 8, at about 2:05 P.M., three Israeli jets strafed the ship; moments later, a trio of torpedo boats joined the attack. Then, as suddenly as it had begun, the action was over, leaving in its wake thirty-four Americans dead or dying and another seventy-five*

twelve hits. Within the laager, one man had been killed and four wounded.

At 0900 Shadmi got orders from Yoffe to build up three task forces for movement west to the Suez Canal. He refused to let Bar-Am's battalion be drawn into this; that frazzled outfit was ordered back to Bir Tamada for what is called regrouping. Yoffe well understood that it had reached the end of the tether. At midnight, getting an inkling that a cease-fire was coming, he had directed the second brigade to be ready to relieve the first brigade by 0300. One battalion of the second was to proceed through Mitla Pass as soon as possible after first light, shunting aside such wreckage as blocked the road. A second battalion would take the southwest road leading to Ras Sudar on Suez. The third battalion would take over the block at the east end of the Pass.

At 0600 Yoffe learned that the second brigade was still not in motion. With that news, he choked up. He started to ask: "Why?" and his voice failed completely. It was time to suck another grapefruit. The battalion sent through Mitla Pass did not reach the western end until dusk on Thursday, 8 June. There it ran into a line of armor, two companies of 54's and 55's drawn up for battle. The Israeli commander ordered his tanks to turn on their lights and charge straight ahead. The Egyptians did not pause to await the movement; whirling about, without firing a round, they sped west, leaving the road to Suez open.

Bar-Am's outfit, after a few hours rest for the men and resupplying of the vehicles at Bir Tamada, was sent on west via the Wadi Gidy. Midway through the defile, Bar-Am was engaged by Egyptian tanks firing from behind rock cover. He broke through their line and went on, reaching the Suez Canal on Thursday evening. Shadmi followed along shortly, was ambushed at the same point, lost one Centurion and four men, and drew off. On Friday morning Yoffe joined him and they went through the Wadi Gidy together, reaching the canal at noon. By then Yoffe had detachments at three points along the water—at Chalufa, Ras Sudar, and on the Little Bitter Lake.

After the cease-fire, feeling safe enough, although he carried no weapon, Yoffe started out in his half-track from Chalufa to see how things were going at Ras Sudar. Halfway, he came upon seven Egyptian T-54's. The crews watched him approach, tried to set their tanks afire, then bounded away. He claims the seven tanks to his personal credit. Living on tea, oranges, and grapefruit—his kit otherwise consisting of water bottle, field glasses, and skin cream—in the five days he had lost fifteen pounds.

The division's losses were less acceptable—twenty tanks, twelve of them repaired by his fighters before they turned home; thirty-four men dead; and sixty-eight wounded. For this they had killed somewhere between one hundred fifty and one hundred eighty enemy tanks. With Division Yoffe as with the others in this action, there is an interesting statistic: although only four per cent of Israel's people live in the kibbutzim, soldiers from the frontier villages had taken twenty-five per cent of the casualties.

On Saturday Yoffe regrouped his two brigades—one at Bir Tamada, the other at Mitla Pass. On Sunday they were alerted for movement home. On Monday morning one brigade mounted a parade at Bir Tamada and was reviewed by the Chief of Staff, General Rabin. On Tuesday the second brigade was reviewed at Mitla Pass by the Prime Minister. By Wednesday, 14 June, the division, back in Israel, was demobilized, and the men, including Yoffe, were all civilians again.

Jerusalem

In Jerusalem in the early morning of 5 June, Brigadier General Uzi Narkis, chief of the Central Command, almost reconciled himself to a war in which his own role would be mainly passive and time-marking. His mind made negative calculations, few of which proved accurate.

In concluding that Jordan would not give battle, but rather that King Hussein's army would make only a token show of force to honor the contract with Nasser, Narkis erred in high company—the Prime Minister, the Minister of Defense, the Chief of Staff, the Chief of Intelligence, and many others were of the same opinion.

Having spent forty-two years in the environs of the city, Narkis thought he knew the territory and the mind of the nearest Arab neighbor. A Jerusalem-born Sabra, graduate of the École de Guerre, and very much the scholarly soldier, Narkis looked to the east and worried most about what the Iraqis might do when they came up. The high ridges between Jerusalem and Ramallah were all-important, the key to dominance west of the Jordan Valley. The Iraqis might have a go at Mount Scopus, the Israeli enclave in Jordan, and that would also be his problem. Should they try to break through to the sea between Tel Aviv and Haifa, higher command would have to deal with it. But with Jordan there would be no real fight. Thinking of these things, Narkis felt easier about his wife and three children at Zahala within easy gun range of Jordan's western border.

On 1 June there had arrived in Amman an Egyptian general, Abdul Munim Riad, to ride herd on Hussein and hold him to his contract, a task he performed too persuasively. Although the mission was secret, Israeli intelligence intercepted news of the arrival; however, it did not get all that the visit implied. Riad, later to be named Egyptian Chief of Staff, was there to regulate the movement of Iraqi forces into Jordan. Three infantry brigades and one of armor, amounting to a reinforced division, had started on their way. (They did not make Jordan in time to do anything but squat in the valley north of Jericho.) When the Iraqis proved too slow, Riad would have two Egyptian commando battalions airlifted from Cairo to deploy into the Jordan West Bank as the battle began. None of these developments were divined from Riad's presence either by Narkis or by G-2, and Israel did not take in dead earnest the threat from the east.

The intelligence estimate was that Jordanian forces would shell two airfields, possibly try to pinch out a third, and might stage a wasting attack toward Mount Scopus, at the very worst. With the Iraqis on his mind, Narkis fretted most about Scopus. If the Iraqis were to conquer that battlement, it would fire up the Jordanians, and the blow to Israel's prestige would be a serious one.

Narkis' task was to defend within his sector, stop any penetration, and counterattack only if key ground were lost. As late as Sunday, 4 June, Dayan had said to him: "You'll be carrying out the mission if you do nothing to provoke Hussein. If his people fire, take it easy; keep silent." So the command was not loaded toward an undreamed opportunity that would wholly transpose the postwar possessing of Palestine. One third of Narkis' small headquarters force were reservists, as were all his troops—three infantry battalions, one mechanized battalion, and some home guard oddments peculiar to a country in which every kibbutz is prepared to stand like a makeshift rifle company.

Yet there was an anchor to windward that had been there since 1 June, when the Egyptian general flew to Amman. In assembly at Ben Shaman east of Tel Aviv was a brigade of armor commanded by Colonel Uri Ben-Ari. A forty-two-year-old tanker and hero of the 1956 war, Ben-Ari had been separated from the regular army for ten years, had achieved success in the publishing business, but was still hurting for a chance to restore a slightly blemished reputation in the army. Ben-Ari and brigade were pointed toward whatever threat might develop along the coastal plain. But if the real thing came against Scopus, the obvious counter was to turn this force toward the ridge-line of Nebi Samwil and the heights around Ramallah. From there he could sweep toward Jerusalem. The hazard of that tentative decision taken on 1 June was clear enough. Ben-Ari's possible target area was anything but tank country. The scarp was high, and the slopes were formidably steep and everywhere rock-walled and rock-rimmed. Once over the border, the armor would be moving directly against long-built fortifications, uphill into a line of rock-walled trenches studded with concrete pillboxes and heavy with anti-tank guns. By day it would be deadly; by night traversable ground would be indistinguishable from a deadfall. While his troops trained, Ben-Ari had four

Jordanian soldiers of the British-trained Arab Legion prepared for action with the confidence of a highly skilled, well-equipped army. In the photograph at top left, Jordanians test equipment in a mobile communications unit on the day before the outbreak of war. At top right, Jordan's thirty-one-year-old ruler, King Hussein I (standing), studies a situation chart with a member of his staff. Opposite, the aftermath of war: Jordanian trucks and demolished military equipment litter a road through the Judean Hills.

88

Seen through the bubble top of his helicopter, Colonel Uri Ben-Ari

days in which to study the map and get the feel of a wholly unfamiliar terrain.

Narkis had one last hunch. The Jordanians might try to take the U.N.-occupied Government House as a gesture. It had been dear to both sides in 1948. So if it came to that and he was ordered to counterattack, he would go on to the village of Sur Bahar, an extension of the ridge from Ramat Rahel, thus cutting the main road between Jerusalem and Bethlehem. It was a passing thought that came and went; he was certain Hussein would not fight all out.

That view changed quickly when zero hour on 5 June came. Immediately Radio Amman crackled with news of the fighting in Sinai, much of it exhortatory. Small arms fire came out of Jordan's side of the divided city. At 0830 the army of Jordan began barraging with artillery and mortars all along the front. Radio reports came to Narkis of civilians getting hit in Jerusalem, Netanya, and elsewhere. Shells from the Jordan Long Toms on the heights exploded into Zahala, and Narkis' family went to the trenches. For one hour Israel's soldiers made no reply (in fact, the Israeli command continued radio silence until past noon). At 1030—exactly one hour before it happened—Narkis heard Radio Amman boast that the Jordanians had taken Government House.

He called General Rabin: "What about counterattacking?" Rabin said: "Go ahead." By noontime two companies of Jordanians were sitting on Government House and a battalion of Colonel Amitai's Israelis was moving east to wrest it away. The shelling of Israel's borderland intensified, with Mount Scopus getting the worst of it.

Through the late morning Narkis pressed for Ben-Ari's brigade. At last the higher command listened. The whole problem was changing. Jordanian pressure was building against the one Israeli military air base to the north. The Jordanian artillery pounding the base was hard against the border. So the Northern Command had been authorized to attack around Jenin and silence the guns. Once Jordan's soil was invaded, there could be no holding back.

Given the brigade, Narkis told Ben-Ari: "I want you to be astride the main road, Ramallah to Jerusalem by 0600 tomorrow morning." Ben-Ari received the formal order in the early afternoon. It read very simply: "Get control of the strategic area around Jerusalem." At the same time there was posted to Central Command a battalion, then a brigade, of paratroopers, who had been due to drop into Sinai; from within the city they would fight toward Scopus and link up with Ben-Ari coming from the north. The commander, Colonel "Motta" Gur, who had stormed Mitla Pass in 1956, got to Jerusalem early Monday afternoon for his briefing. Narkis said to him: "You are to attack the Police School; you must keep in mind the Old City." Gur's battalion came up from Tel Aviv on civilian buses to Jerusalem, arriving at 1900, after a three-hour haul. Finally Narkis was having big dreams and getting the shape of things to come. He called Mayor Teddy Kollek and said: "It has begun; you will be the Mayor of a united Jerusalem." His Honor said: "All right, all right, all right."

By then elements of the Jerusalem brigade were sitting on Sur Bahar, after driving off one company of Jordanians. The fight for Government House, concluded at 1530, had cost ten lives. The new city continued under heavy shellfire. General Dayan, heading the one ministry to be based in Tel Aviv, arrived in Jerusalem to take his oath of office. The ceremony had to be

Text continued on page 95.

Displaying the symbolic "V" and an upside-down portrait of King Hussein, Israeli soldiers in the crowded jeep above proclaim victory after their rout of Jordan on June 7. At a press conference in Amman twelve days later, the defeated Jordanian king (right) appeared before newsmen in the uniform and field marshal's insignia he wore throughout the fighting. Stressing the need to "start along new lines," he called for a closer Arab unity and "a new approach" to Arab problems.

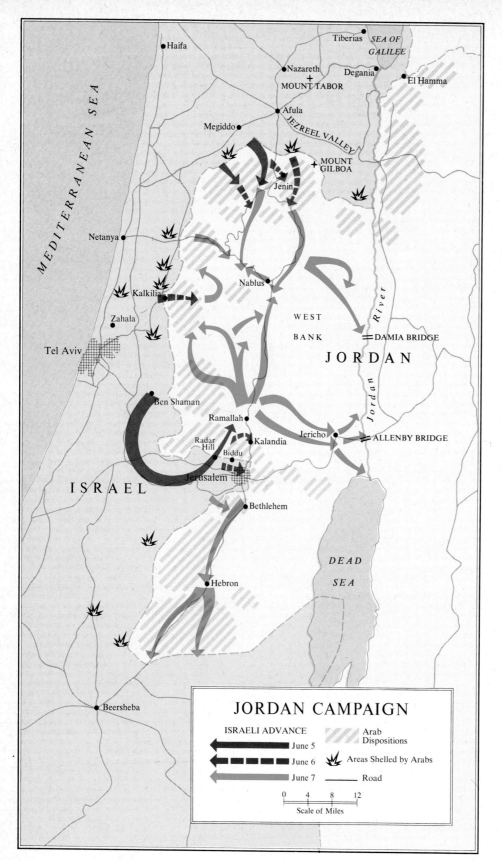

At the outbreak of war on Monday, June 5, Israel's Central Command in Jerusalem expected Jordanian participation to be limited to token support for the Arab cause. When it became clear late that morning that the bombardment of Israeli settlements was more than a gesture, Israel retaliated in a three-day campaign that swept Jordan's West Bank (see map at left). As Northern Command units advanced toward the heights of Jenin on Monday, an armored brigade battled for the high ground between Jerusalem and Ramallah to the south. On Wednesday, Israeli forces closed in on Nablus, drove east to Jericho and the Jordan River, and captured Bethlehem and Hebron in the south. By Wednesday evening the Jordanian army was defeated, and Israel controlled all the area west of the Jordan River.

A casualty of the 1967 fighting, as it had been of the 1948–49 war, the Church of the Dormition atop Israel's Mount Zion lost its roof to flames. Through its exposed frame (opposite), Israeli observers had an unexcelled view of Jordan's Old City. The Romanesque church covers the site where Mary, the Mother of Jesus, is said to have fallen asleep before being raised to heaven. Nearby, also on the sacred hill, is the room of the Last Supper and King David's tomb.

canceled because of the bombardment. Mrs. Dayan had gone early in the day to Jerusalem on private business, intending to tarry and witness the swearing-in. During the bombardment she sought cover in a filling station. When evening came and the affair was canceled, making her long wait futile, she is reported to have chided her husband: "How was I to know your war would start today?"

At 1320 Monday afternoon, Colonel Ben-Ari and brigade had moved toward Jerusalem. A column of armor ultimately stretched twenty miles along the mountain road—one thousand vehicles: half-tracks carrying the armored infantry, World War II Shermans forming the bulk of his tank strength, with one company of Centurions in the van charged with a nigh-impossible mission.

Four hours and thirty miles farther along, he was on the high ground, just beyond the kibbutz Maa Leh Hahamisha, peering through darkness at the fortified ridges of Jordan and disposing of his forces for a quick go at them. The time was about 1720 when he got his first twenty-eight tanks set in their fire positions.

The plan that had taken shape in his mind, the opening phase of which he was about to execute, stemmed from the order: "Get control of the strategic area of Jerusalem." That could only mean going for the high ground to the north of the Holy City, in particular the key piece of it, Tel-el-Full (Bean Hill), where King Hussein's summer palace was under construction.

But between where he stood and the objective were two formidable bastions, Radar Hill, just across the line from Maa Leh Hahamisha, and Sheikh-

As Israelis complete the encircle-ment of Jordanian Jerusalem on Wednesday, a sniper (opposite) trains his rifle on the Tomb of Absalom, an Arab outpost on the Jericho Road. Above, an Israeli patrol takes up position at the Dung Gate, inside the Old City's southern wall. A wounded man on a stretcher awaits medical attention.

OVERLEAF: *A column of Israeli infantry follows a tank along a road outside Jordanian Jerusalem. The hillside road running from right to center leads up Mount Scopus, since 1949 a Jewish enclave in Arab territory. The bombed-out farm at left formerly held an Arab garrison.*

95

Abdul-Aziz, about five miles to the east of it. Here were the only passes through the mountains into Jordan, and Jordan's army had dug and delved for twenty years to bar passage. One mountain road, rough and rock-strewn, pointed toward each, and there were no other possible approaches. The road stopped at the border. Beyond its terminus was the hill, thick with concrete blockhouses, troop billets and pillboxes, all connected by a trench system with shellproof head cover. Forward of this reticulation was a wired-in mine field two hundred or so meters across, skirted by a twelve-foot-deep anti-tank ditch.

Sheikh-Abdul-Aziz was fortified in just about the same way. Since one position looked no less nasty than the other, Ben-Ari had already parted his two battalions of Shermans. They would attack simultaneously, one going against each hill. The honor of the brigade was more than a little at stake in this affair. In 1948, when Ben-Ari was a captain, it had also attacked Radar Hill. He now placed himself with the column on the left to make certain that this time it would bull through.

An extra piece of insurance, the company of Centurions had tracked on farther up the mountain. There is a place called Beit Kika, not a fortified place, for there is no need of man-made works, since nature shaped these ridges to defy anything on wheels or tracks. A trace runs through it and loops over the ridges—proof that living things have gone that way from time to time, possibly goats. No horseman would take it; the way is too steep, the trace too narrow, the boulders too loose and too many. Ben-Ari thought there was a chance that the Centurions might make the grade. He had been optimistic ever since first told that he would not have to sit out the war. That he was playing a long, long shot he well understood. He was prepared to lose tanks to the terrain, and if any squeaked through, he might still be ahead.

The battle against Radar Hill, as at Sheikh-Abdul-Aziz, began at 1930. The reinforced company of Jordanians manning Radar Hill (the garrison at Aziz was the same size) had no tanks in support; its heaviest fires came from ten antitank guns. For twenty-five minutes Ben-Ari's armor shelled the position with armor-piercing rounds, concentrating on the antitank guns. The same was done at Aziz. On signal from Ben-Ari, these fires lifted; and on

both fronts two companies of armored infantry worked through the mine fields and stormed into the works. On Radar Hill the hand-to-hand fighting in the rock-walled trenches went on for seventeen minutes; at Aziz it lasted longer. It was tooth-and-nail in the dark; the Jordanians would not quit.

When this deadly grapple ended, Ben-Ari had lost no tanks at either position. But the checkup showed twenty infantrymen killed and eighty-one wounded. The casualties had to be hand-carried down the rear slope to the waiting ambulances; the evacuation was conducted under preregistered artillery and mortar barrage fires.

Then came the back-breaking grind of coping with the mine fields and other obstacles so that the tanks could ride through. Engineers did much of the clearing, assisted by demolition squads from the armored infantry. To the latter fell the less dangerous and more wearing task of making a road through the tank ditch by filling it in with rock and rubble. All of this labor done in darkness was unaided by machines. Eight hours passed, and 0200, Tuesday morning, was at hand before Ben-Ari could give the order to move again. Even so, that passage was a hard rub. Eight tanks—Shermans stripped of tracks or losing a bogie wheel—were temporarily lost during the lurch forward. Some mines had been missed. Next day they were running again, thanks to the repair crews within the units doing the fighting.

Ben-Ari was hearing the news on radio from the one company trying to break through on the high line around Beit Kika. It was mournful. In nine hours the Centurions had made less than two miles. Now twelve of them were definitely stranded, snagged on their bellies by the boulders. The other eighteen were still struggling forward, a few feet at a time.

Beyond Sheikh-Abdul-Aziz was another fortified position, Biddu, named for the village next to it. The right-hand column hit it at once. The defenders were popping flares all over the place, thus making a gift of a fully illuminated objective to Ben-Ari's people. For that reason only, it was shorter work than at Aziz, although a full Jordanian company defended the position. Still, Ben-Ari left behind five more killed and twenty wounded from the one company of Shermans that had assaulted. He also dropped off one battalion to police the whole area and cover his rear.

A sequence of photographs taken from the back of a jeep (from left to right above) shows the quick movement around and into the Old City. Pausing at the northeast corner of the walls (with Jordan's Archaeological Museum rising behind them to the right), an Israeli group receives its instructions. With the wall to its right (second picture), the vehicle moves down a deserted road. Swinging his camera around, the photographer captures a second jeep passing a burning bus. Having entered the Old City through St. Stephen's Gate, the group approaches the Dome of the Rock.

The others moved on east to Nebi Samwil, the highest and most beautiful ridge in this part of Jordan, according to tradition the ground where the Prophet Samuel was buried. Ben-Ari led the way in a half-track. The platoon of Arab snipers in position along the crest fired a few shots and then fled.

At 0400, as dawn of 6 June cracked, the brigade cut the main road between Ramallah and Jerusalem, and Ben-Ari could say that he had completed his mission. About then there came to him the eighteen Centurions that had managed to wiggle through the rocks at Beit Kika, leaving twelve dropouts behind to show that the task was not easy. The brigade was feeling stronger all the time. It had also been joined in early morning by a company of AML's, armored cars with 90-mm. guns.

After a quick regrouping the brigade, having tried for Tel-el-Full, assaulted Tel Zahara, another high knob on the opposite side of the main road and four hundred meters to the west; at last, forces stood solidly positioned on high ground covering the highway from one flank. It was done in the nick

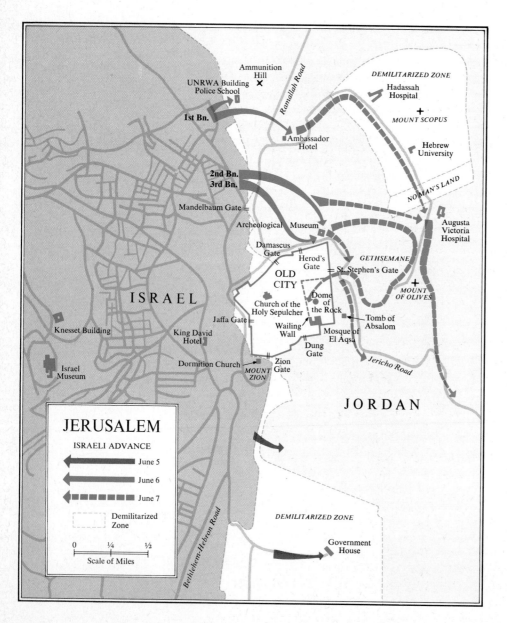

As Jordanian shelling intensified along the Demilitarized Zone between old and new Jerusalem on the morning of June 5, the Israeli Central Command prepared for battle. Jordan's capture of Government House triggered the first action (see map at left), and by early afternoon the building was in Israeli hands. Early next morning three Israeli battalions advanced to the north in a move to take the high ground and clear the way for capture of the Old City. On June 7, Israeli soldiers broke through St. Stephen's Gate, reached the Wailing Wall, and took possession of the Holy City. The same day all of Jerusalem fell to Israel.

of time. There came on immediately a heavy task force of Jordanians via the road from Jericho—twenty Patton tanks and lorried infantry. The battle lasted three hours, breaking off at 0800 with the retreat of eight Pattons toward Jericho, leaving the other twelve burning on the battlefield. Protracting the engagement, the Jordanians had tried to fight their tanks from behind the houses of the neighborhood, which made them fleeting targets. The advantage of high ground and better shooting determined the issue. The brigade had lost no tanks, although four of its half-tracks had been knocked out.

Ben-Ari had commanded from an eminence that is known as the Castle. Looking now, he decided that the brigade as deployed was much too congested. So he flew by chopper to Zahara and from there directed an attack on Tel-el-Full. By 0830 that hill was in his hands. The assault had cost him two of the AML's, but the brigade had killed three more Pattons.

At 0900 came orders by radio that he should move south and link up with forces in the north of Jerusalem. Two more defended Jordanian strong points stood in his way—the Hill of the Split Road just beyond the town of Swafat and French Hill, which is hard by Mount Scopus. They had to be taken, and it was done with armored shock, the tanks charging straight on to overrun both positions. The resistance centered in fifteen antitank guns and about double that number of 105 recoilless rifles.

Lasting less than two hours, it was a bloody go. Ben-Ari lost two Sher-

Crouching in front of a dead Arab, Israelis guard a disputed intersection in Jerusalem.

101

Wary of Arab snipers, the Israeli at left hides behind an oil drum as his comrades flatten themselves by tank traps in the street. Above, a tank moves through a city street, while the soldiers below dash down a narrow Jerusalem passageway.

mans, three half-tracks, ten dead, and thirty-one wounded. Such was the impact on the forces that, with the fight half done, he felt forced to recall troops to Swafat to get squared around for another try. They went on again; to their amazement, the hill was empty. The Jordanians had fled.

Later he would brood over this fight, and for several reasons. Between his troops and the objective was a built-up area of houses, flats, and stores. Shells bounced off solid rock walls; the clatter and roar of the exchange were many times amplified. Swafat was like a place of the dead, just the wrong setting for battle. Then midway of the encounter, the men around him were strafed by one of their own planes. His own half-track was hit; another was demolished. Two reconnaissance jeeps also were hit. Soldiers were hit by their own fire. At the climax the two sides had slugged it out fifty to one hundred meters apart. Glad when it ended, Ben-Ari led his men straight south. In less than ten minutes the brigade's front element entered Jerusalem and linked up with Colonel Gur's people.

At 1400, Tuesday afternoon, higher command ordered him to turn about and capture Ramallah. He was told another column out of Northern Command would be coming toward him from Latrun and that he should wait in Ramallah for the juncture. So he figured that one battalion—about forty

tanks—would be enough for the task. They barreled straight in along the main road, firing as they moved. To his surprise, hundreds of snipers were firing from the windows and housetops. Machine guns also were popping away from the near ridge-tops. More surprising still, all of that fire went silent when his vehicles came to the central square. This had happened at 1830, with only thirty minutes of daylight remaining. One of his units broke into some Jordanian military stores and lifted ten trumpets. Staying the night there seemed too risky. One battalion bivouacked north of Ramallah in open country, the other at Kalandia airfield.

At 0700, on 7 June, Ben-Ari was ordered to attack north to Nablus, but the order was canceled thirty minutes later; one battalion would go north, the other two would strike for Jericho. They moved east down the ridges over two dirt roads. By 1030 they were three miles from Jericho, below sea level, but still descending. Waiting for them on the flat ground, seven hundred feet below, was an Arab force of twenty Patton tanks. The situation

Guarded by a single Israeli, a line of Arab prisoners (opposite) marches up the stairs to the Dome of the Rock. After the surrender of the Old City an Arab waving a white flag (above) approaches the Dung Gate. Not all Jews hailed the capture of the Old City; members of an extreme Hasidic sect oppose the secular Israeli state and await the Messiah to liberate their holy places from the Arabs. Below, left, an old man hands out leaflets denouncing the war. The woman below, right, welcomes the Israeli conquerors to the Old City.

could not have been more favorable. Right then—at 1039—Ben-Ari was ordered to get back to Ramallah. The brigade turned back uphill. At 1200, orders were changed. "Be ready to move either north to Nablus or south to Hebron." At 1300 came another order: turn about and capture Jericho. The brigade swung about. All these false stops and starts, the swiveling of battalions on goat tracks, had put another fifty-five miles on the tanks.

By 1830, Wednesday afternoon, the brigade front was a little more than a mile short of Jericho. The Jordanian tankers had run off, leaving fifteen otherwise sound Pattons stuck in the mud of the banana plantations. At 1830 the last Israeli attack started. One mixed battle group headed for the police station. Another went straight for the center of the city with all guns blazing. (The Jordanians were still replying with the fire of Long Toms and one battalion of 105-mm. self-propelled howitzers.) As the column raced in, ten of Ben-Ari's soldiers broke out the ten liberated trumpets and blasted away; and the last wall of resistance tumbled down.

It was exactly 1900 when the last shots died away at Jericho. To the west, where the ridges rose terracelike from the Dead Sea to Jerusalem, a narrow strip of sky was still feebly light. Ben-Ari looked that way and said: "We made it just in time; no need to order the moon up."

There remained other chores. The Allenby, Abdullah, and Shoarat bridges had to be blown, which was done the following day. Already the road from Jerusalem was jammed with thousands of refugees trekking east, many for reasons that they themselves did not understand. One battalion set up stations to provide them with water, food, and medical care. Ten minutes after the last shot was fired, Ben-Ari saw his soldiers turn into social workers.

Four of his tanks had been lost beyond repair. Of his thirty-six men killed, seven had been officers. He said to himself only that it was that many too many.

As the May crisis lengthened, Colonel Mordechai Gur, a thirty-seven-year-old regular who commanded Israel's Command and General Staff School, had been shifted from that seat to command a paratroop brigade he had not seen before.

Except for four other professionals who went with him, the whole brigade was formed of reservists. Even so, as June approached, the force was designated as the general headquarters reserve. If war came, the unit expected to get a drop mission somewhere in Sinai. Accordingly, it was based near one of the airfields north of Tel Aviv, and its gear stayed loaded for an airborne task.

Gur, though a most positive character, has an inquiring mind. It occurred to him that a new war might start with the army of Jordan making a surprise attack on Mount Scopus. Jerusalem was weakly garrisoned, and his brigade might be called to fight there. So on 31 May, on his own initiative, he went to Jerusalem and spent the day looking over the ground.

What he saw convinced him that he should do it again, taking his staff and battalion commanders along. Friends on the General Staff discouraged him, saying: "Don't waste time. No one is worrying about Jerusalem. Continue to study Sinai." So he desisted, which proved to be a mistake.

When, on the morning of 5 June, he heard that the Jordanian army was shelling the New City, he concluded it was not his business; all brigade equip-

Among the early visitors to the captured Old City was David Ben-Gurion, revered first Prime Minister of Israel. Above, nearly dwarfed by soldiers eager to show him the long-denied sights of Arab Jerusalem, the white-haired octogenarian visits the Dome of the Rock on June 8. Sacred to Jews as the site of their destroyed Temple, the Moslem mosque also covers the spot from which Mohammed is said to have ascended to heaven. The jubilant soldiers opposite, having just seized the Dome on June 7, wave Israeli flags and captured Arab banners.

ment stayed loaded or bundled for a drop into Sinai. Then came the call to send one battalion to Jerusalem. He went on ahead of it, to talk to General Narkis; by late afternoon the two of them had agreed on a tentative plan. Both knew by then that all of Colonel Gur's paratroop brigade had been ordered up to the city.

Narkis was not yet thinking of a general assault against Jordan, all along the West Bank. They did not even discuss it. Gur proposed to concentrate against the built-up area of the city, moving first against the Rockefeller Archaeological Museum, a jump-off point for the Old City. This objective captured, he could enter via Herod's Gate and from Sheikh-Jerach advance to the American and Vadi Jos quarters. Narkis approved, and that was as far as they went. Whether there would be a second phase, and what form it would take, would depend on the success or failure of Ben-Ari's brigade to the north.

This done, Gur, his staff, and senior commanders called by headquarters of the Jerusalem brigade to pick up maps and photos needed in the operation. It was being heavily pounded by artillery, and they cleared away as quickly as possible—Gur to set up a temporary command post at 72 Tsfania Street, because there was good observation from the roof. Then for several hours, while it was still daylight, and the commanders could get forward to see the target areas, they worked out what they would do. Gur planned to penetrate the Jordanian army's fixed defenses at two points with battalion-size attacks—one near the Police School (UNRWA building), the other near Sheikh-Jerach tomb. After the breakthrough the third battalion would follow along on the Sheikh-Jerach line, and all three battalions would mop up in assigned sectors. The first battalion's zone would include the Police School, Ammunition Hill, and the Hotel Ambassador; the second battalion's zone was around the Archaeological Museum and the American and Vadi Jos quarters; the third battalion was to clear the road to Herod's Gate and capture the Archaeological Museum.

At 1700 the commander of the one tank company out of the Jerusalem brigade that would support Gur came by to be briefed on the planning; he got away in a hurry so that he could scout the ground where the two battalions would jump off.

By 2000 Monday evening, half an hour after the last light faded, the troops began to arrive in public buses, the column having come up the main road from the coastal plain. To Gur's astonishment, many of the junior officers and most of the soldiers knew nothing of Jerusalem. It was too late to look; so they were given a quick schooling about the streets and buildings where they would shortly be engaged. Worse yet, the brigade was arriving almost empty-handed, its gear still loaded at the airfield for the drop into Sinai that never came off. For the next hour there was a great scurrying about by Gur and his staff to borrow arms, ammunition, and other essentials from the reserve stores of the Jerusalem brigade. At 2130 General Narkis talked to Gur, and they agreed that the attack should start around midnight. Soon after, Colonel Amitai attached to Gur's brigade, as a reserve, one of his battalions that had been fighting in line all day.

At 2230, Gur returned to his command post, to be told by his deputy: "We can't possibly start by midnight; some units still have no supply." H-hour was put off until 0100 on Tuesday, 6 June. One-half hour later Lieuten-

Brigadier General Uzi Narkis (left) with Colonel Mordechai Gur.

ant Colonel Moshe Peres, who was forward with the troops, called again to say: "We cannot get ready by an hour from now, and for the same reason." Gur lay down for a cat nap. General Narkis then called Peres to suggest that it might be better to delay the attack until dawn. Every officer around Peres objected. At 0200 all three battalions reported to Peres: "We are ready." By then Colonel Gur had moved his command post to a more central point on Yoel Street, where he would stay until the Archaeological Museum was finally captured.

At 0215 the artillery opened fire on the target areas. The tanks moved into position to shell the routes of penetration. When the barrage lifted, and from that time through the next seven and one-half hours, the attacking battalions carried the full burden. Gur and his staff literally had nothing to do. Units in the assault hardly bothered to report; they kept hacking away on their missions according to plan.

Yet in that fight the brigade lost one of every five soldiers—seventy-five killed and three hundred wounded. Many of these fell before they put a foot on enemy soil, hit by artillery, mortar fragments, and bullets as they crawled toward the barricaded trenches that covered the Police Barracks. The battalion attacking toward the Archaeological Museum lost the equivalent of one company before it could form a fire line. The evacuation of the worst-hit cases, done under continuous fire, further crippled the battalion. Somehow the movement managed to press slowly on. Breakthrough—the crashing of the Jordanian army's mined, wired, and entrenched front—took almost two hours.

All that while the fighting swirled and flamed around the Police School and Ammunition Hill. Soon after dawn on Tuesday the worst was over. The engineers cleared a lane through the mines and wire in front of the Police School, and the tank company moved through without loss. Two of the companies fighting on Ammunition Hill, one led by Captain Dedi, the other by Captain Dodik, mustered less than a platoon when the fight died. Sixty Jordanians had been killed on the hill; Israel lost thirty-six men.

As day came on, Gur stopped all artillery firing against the built-up area and directed the one tank company to spread out and place one platoon with each rifle battalion. Major Ouzi's second battalion was being hard-pressed by snipers from the windows and housetops of the American Quarter and Lieutenant Yoske's third battalion was losing too many men to the same kind of fire around the Mandelbaum Gate. The Jordanian artillery was shelling both routes with extremely accurate fire. Trying to go too fast, the small groups doing the fighting were passing up too many houses. It was no good; too many soldiers were being shot from the rear. Gur put a brake on the movement. At about 0900 with both battalions reaching for the Archaeological Museum, he started the forward shift of his command post to work out the second phase of the operation. How soon it could begin would depend upon the arrival of Ben-Ari, who was still fighting hard around the Hill of the Split Road near Swafat.

Visiting the Police School thirty minutes later, Gur realized for the first time how crippling were his losses. The brigade casualty figures were woeful enough. Then Captain Raffi, the tank commander, told him that every tank commander had been hit; the tanks were down to one shell apiece; and half the armor was no longer mobile. A repair shop was set up in the Police

School yard. One of Ben-Ari's tank companies was put at Gur's disposal by General Narkis. But that company had also suffered heavily and was not yet south of French Hill. Losses within Gur's battalions were replaced out of Amitai's Jerusalem brigade. Sizing all things up, Gur knew that he was stopped for a while. It was time to throttle down and rest the brigade. For some of the men the high pressure eased off until sundown.

Still, the picture around the perimeter of the Holy City kept on shifting in Israel's favor—and with it, the political prospect grew brighter. By midmorning some of Ben-Ari's people and some of Gur's had joined hands in north Jerusalem, although the commanders did not see one another. The link-up opened the way to Mount Scopus. Tel Karen, in the extreme extension of the West Bank bulge, was taken by another reserve infantry brigade under the central command. At noon General Dayan arrived in Jerusalem and went with Narkis to Mount Scopus; troops who did not know their own commanding general by sight still cheered lustily when the war minister came in view, thanks to the eye patch. There on Mount Scopus, Dayan told Narkis to cut through Jerusalem from the east, a movement that called for the capture of Augusta Victoria Hospital, the Mount of Olives, and Izaria, a Jordanian village slightly down the slope. One of Gur's battalions was put on the task. Promptly, it began losing men. Narkis told Gur to knock it off. Things were coming his way. Why press?

The night of 6–7 June in Jerusalem was made for forays, alarms, and confusions. Amitai's troops that had taken Government House went way out to capture Deir Agu Tor, a Jordanian village overlooking the Holy City. At 1830, Gur's brigade started on the second phase, the capture of the eastern hills. After taking all day to refit, the tanks showed up at 1900, and it was already dark. Gur led them to the wall, where he pointed the way. One company under Captain Aitan was to provide a covering fire for the attack by the second battalion; the other was to advance directly against Augusta Victoria, the battalion objective.

In the dark, Captain Raffi lost his way, made the wrong turn, got on the main road to Jericho, and ran into intense artillery fire. He called on radio to Gur: "Somehow I've missed; tell me where I am." Gur asked him: "What do you see around you?" Raffi read off the signs. Gur, a Jerusalem-born Sabra who knew the city like his own backyard, recognized nothing. He could not imagine that Raffi had strayed so far afield.

Gur dispatched Major Capusta of the reconnaissance unit to look for Raffi. Capusta scouted forward for a distance, then returned to instruct one of his platoon commanders how to proceed with the search. The unit set forth. Minutes passed. Gur heard cries on his radio: "Doctor, doctor, please doctor." It was the voice of the platoon commander. For better or worse, he too had missed the turn, wheeled onto the Jericho road, come under heavy

After the capture of the Jordanian sector of Jerusalem, the Wailing Wall, all that remains of the Second Temple, became the scene of zealous celebration. At right, an Israeli soldier joins a group of ecstatic Hasidim, members of an ultra-orthodox sect, to dance an impromptu hora.

fire from the wall, and gotten himself, his people, and his jeeps well riddled.

Out of the second error, Gur at last understood what had happened. He told his G-2 (intelligence officer), Major Arik: "Go to the Jericho road and bring back Raffi's tanks." His G-3 (staff officer for operations), Major Amos, was told to take Aitan's company and replace Raffi's company for the assault on Augusta Victoria hill. The second battalion under Ouzi was ordered to proceed with the mission.

All this was in vain. Gur started toward the scene of the impending action. On his way he heard from General Narkis on radio that a strong force of Jordanian armor (forty Pattons) was coming along the Jericho road; Gur's entire brigade should fold back into a defensive position.

These things happened shortly before midnight, Tuesday. Jordan's Pattons were indeed coming on. Figuring Gur's people were too worn down to brace against tanks, Narkis asked for an air strike on the Jericho road. The planes came over, dropped many flares, then reported that they had hit and stopped the armor. It was another mistake of the night. They had strafed, instead, a battalion of 25-pounder artillery. But indirectly the air strike had done its work. Wanting none of it, the armor turned about. By that time the tanks of Ben-Ari's brigade were already threatening Jericho through the back door.

At 0500 on 7 June, Narkis got this word from the high command: "You must move as quickly as possible and take the Old City. A cease-fire is coming fast."

The message altered all calculations. Narkis had set 1100 as the time for the operation he had discussed with Dayan the day before. He now brought it forward two hours. At 0830 Wednesday the air force put a telling strike on the main target. At 0900 Gur's troops captured Izaria and at 0945, they broke through St. Stephen's Gate (also called the Lion's Gate). Gur was first in his half-track. Ten minutes later they had arrived at the Dome of the Rock.

At 1010, Narkis, moving in his own half-track, joined Gur at the Wailing Wall. What great words are said by simple soldiers in such high moments? Narkis remarked: "It's fantastic." Gur answered: "To be here, yes." There were about two hundred troops with Gur at the Wall, and fire from snipers was kicking up dirt and bouncing from the rock all about.

Fighting on quite a different line, the Jerusalem brigade was at the same time occupying the ground from Mount Zion to the east for one-half mile, to assist the advance of Gur's forces. The tanks under Aitan attacked straight up the slope of Augusta Victoria, which stands almost as high as Mount Scopus. By 1030 one of Gur's battalions was at the Mosque of Omar. Shortly after noon, all Jerusalem was under Israel's control. Soon after 1600, Amitai's brigade turned toward Bethlehem and Hebron, taking off from Ramat Rahael. Bethlehem was taken just before sundown; there had been little resistance along the road. No fire was directed against the city of Christ's birth and none came forth.

There are few scars from the fighting, on either the Old City or the New. By the hour of the cease-fire, when all of the West Bank was in Israel's hands, most of the rubble had been cleared from the Jerusalem streets, and the wire barricades and mine fields were fast disappearing. Of the two brigades, one hundred twenty-five men had died to make the city whole again.

After taking the Old City of Jerusalem, Israelis bulldozed adjoining buildings that blocked access to their sacred Wailing Wall, thus making room for the multitudes that soon flocked to pray at the site, left. Before the area could be cleared, chief military rabbi Shlomo Goren, his Biblical white beard contrasting strangely with a modern army uniform, stands in the narrow alley at the Wall and leads soldiers in prayer, above. It was the first service since the Arabs sealed off the Old City in 1948. Chanting at the Wall, a youthful Israeli soldier (right) wears a skull cap but no prayer shawl: his shoulders are draped instead with machine-gun bullets.

Hours before the outbreak of full-scale war on the Syrian front, an Israeli helicopter (opposite) airlifts wounded soldiers from border kibbutzim amid shellfire from Syrian emplacements on the heights above. Below, an Israeli gunner sits at his machine-gun post atop a tank moving into Syria.

The Northern Front

Having some knowledge of the Syrians, Israel's high command did not expect them to come down like the wolf on the fold. Still, the manner in which that Arab army, having early and strongly reinforced its fortified front along the Golan Plateau rampart during early May, procrastinated after the war started on 5 June wholly surprised forty-two-year-old Brigadier General David Eleazar, chief of the Northern Command, based on Nazareth. Yugoslavian-born, Israeli-educated, very soft-spoken, Eleazar, like Narkis and Tal, is physically in the lightweight class.

Knowing what they must meet if they tried to move offensively very probably accounted for the Syrian reluctance. The Huleh Valley, below the Golan Plateau, is flat, broad, wide open, and lush. An infantry line attacking across it would be at the mercy of the Israeli artillery on the heights to the west and the tanks in the bottom lands maneuvering around the approaches to the high ground. The Golan Plateau, for all its defensive advantages, was only a springboard to a nigh-coverless battlefield.

The Syrian army stalled. Until 0540 on Tuesday, 6 June, even the artillery was held on leash; ten of the Israeli valley settlements were shelled, and the barraging continued for more than one hour. As the fire dropped off, two Syrian tank companies and one rifle battalion were thrown into a half-organized attack against Kibbutz Dan on the floor of the valley. That clumsy effort was repulsed in thirty minutes, with the loss of seven Syrian tanks and not a few infantrymen. At 1930, 6 June, the same force again went for Dan and was driven back, this time by tank fire only. Being out-gunned, Eleazar was using his artillery only for counterbattery fire. Israel's air force was giving the ground fighters some support, but its weapons had small effect on Syrian

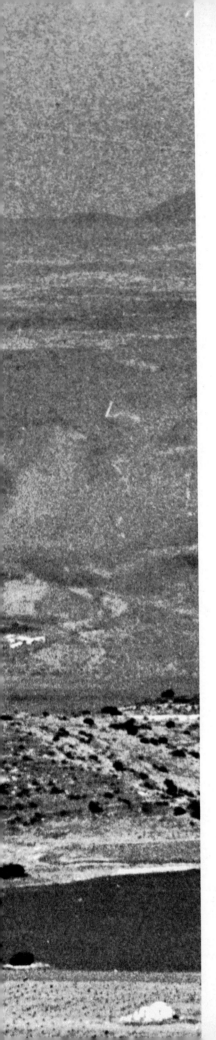

works tunneled along the basalt crests of the Golan Plateau's foothills. Later the same day there was a third thrust toward Dan; it was so weakly done that Eleazar wondered why the Syrians had tried.

Israel's unerring tank-against-tank action decided this incredibly brief fight for the valley, Syria's one spark of offensive spirit. Although the armored force against Syria used Israel's least serviceable tanks so that the best could be thrown against Egypt, it was nevertheless an organization of experts. That was a substantial gain since the 1956 war, in which armor was taken from the dock in Haifa straight to the battlefield under the handling of crews with little knowledge of how to fight tanks. Men like Tal, Adan, and above all, the Deputy Chief of Staff, Brigadier General Haim Barlev, had solidified the corps during the ten years. Now all formations, reserve and standing force, used only soldiers who had spent their thirty months of full-time army duty handling tanks.

Syrian bombardment of the valley settlements lasted through 9 June, with small loss except to property. Two male civilians were killed while walking a road in broad day; women and children stayed in the shelters, the latter probably loving the excitement. Well before the end of the first day of war in the Huleh Valley, General Eleazar had concluded that—although he had only a sprinkling of troops to protect Galilee and its northern extension —he could spare some of his brigades to join the fight against Jordan south of Mount Gilboa. Although he had already resolved to stage only major attacks against Syria, the gesture of actually weakening his forces against that country was the epitome of contempt for it.

Two brigades were shifted south within the first twenty-four hours of the war; the movement, initially, had a purely defensive object. From the northern end of its West Bank, Jordan was shelling Israel's nearby air base, the heliport next to the museum-fortress of Megiddo, and the surrounding settlements. The brigade under Colonel Moshe Bar-Kochva, who in mien and manner is the most leonine fighter in Israel's army, went forth to damper these fires.

By late afternoon of 5 June the brigade was at the border. Eleazar flew there, discussed the plan with his man, and altered it. He decided to enlarge his limited attack on the Jordanian artillery base in order to take the high ground around Jenin at the same time. It was also agreed that one of Bar-Kochva's battalions should move separately, parallel to the main body and farther to the west. In mountain country, when not engaging fortifications, Eleazar thinks it desirable to attack in as many places as possible.

The area assaulted by the brigade was being defended by Jordan's 25th Infantry Brigade and 47th Tank Battalion, which was maneuvering with forty Patton tanks. The attacking brigade had only one battalion of unconverted Shermans. But the gunnery of the Jordanian tankers was bad and their teamplay was worse; the Shermans invariably got off a first round, and usually a second, before the Pattons fired. When the battle for the heights of Jenin ended, just before sundown on 5 June, twenty-one Jordanian Pattons lay burning along the ridges. For Bar-Kochva's brigade the break-in was long

Text continued on page 120.

From their defensive positions on the Golan Plateau the Syrians bombarded Israeli settlements in the fertile Huleh Valley (left) from June 6 through June 9. The Syrian heights rise from below sea level to 1,000 feet in a mile and a half.

117

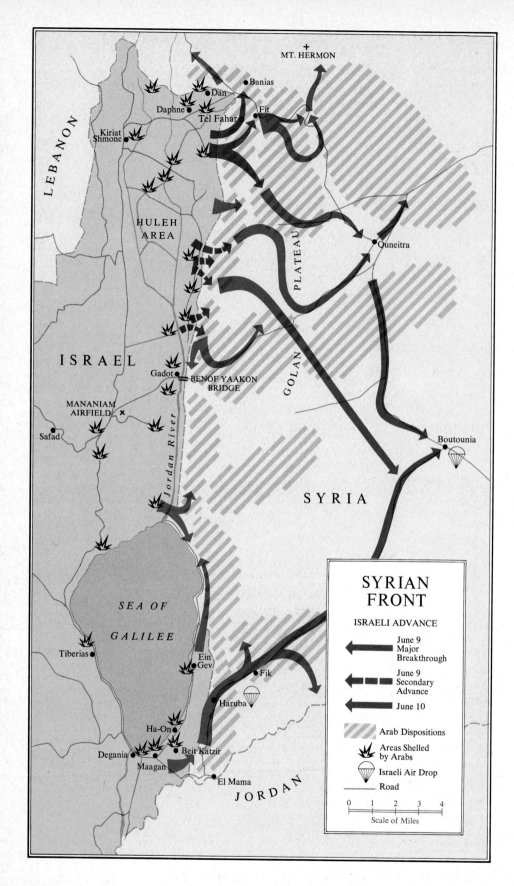

SYRIAN FRONT

ISRAELI ADVANCE

⬅ June 9
Major
Breakthrough

⬅ June 9
Secondary
Advance

⬅ June 10

▨ Arab Dispositions

✹ Areas Shelled
by Arabs

⛊ Israeli Air Drop

Road

0 1 2 3 4
Scale of Miles

Map labels: MT. HERMON, Banias, Dan, Daphne, Fit, Tel Fahar, Kiriat Shmone, LEBANON, HULEH AREA, Quneitra, PLATEAU, GOLAN, ISRAEL, Gadot, BENOF YAAKON BRIDGE, MANANIAM AIRFIELD, Safad, Jordan River, SYRIA, Boutounia, SEA OF GALILEE, Tiberias, Ein Gev, Fik, Haruba, Ha-On, Beit Katzir, Degania, Maagan, El Mama, JORDAN

Brigadier General David Eleazar

During the first four days of war the Syrian effort was confined to small attacks against the Israeli border (shelled areas on map at left). When full-scale fighting erupted on the morning of June 9, Israel's Northern Command focused on the nearly impregnable enemy fortress of Tel Fahar, commanding the Arab-entrenched Golan ridges and the Huleh Valley below. After a fierce, day-long battle the fortress fell—and with it the Syrian army. From there it was mainly a mop-up exercise as Israeli troops pushed east to Quneitra. Syria's acceptance of a cease-fire halted the advance on June 10.

The Syrian outpost of Pawafic—a heavily fortified position overlooking a narrow strip of Israeli territory east of the Sea of Galilee—was one of the most fiercely contested fortifications of the conflict in the north. The photograph at right, taken from a ridge opposite Pawafic, shows a distant shellfire exchange between the Syrian position (at top) and the Israeli kibbutz of Ma'agan only a few yards below.

and costly, the breakthrough was almost unopposed, and the pursuit turned into a rout.

Eleazar heard soon after midnight that the Jordanians were concentrating around Qabateye. Between that town and the Damya Bridge was the 40th Infantry Brigade—two battalions of M-48's and one of armored infantry. To scatter this concentration if possible, he feinted with a column of lorries, a few tanks, and a platoon of mortars toward the Jordan Valley; his troops were instructed to make as much noise as possible. The ruse worked; one battalion of the M-48's was rushed north. The brigade took Qabateye a few hours after dawn on Tuesday, its armor cracking the outer defenses and the infantry battalion capturing the town.

To extend this movement, an armored brigade that had been in defensive position along the Sea of Galilee was already rolling south. It was under the command of Colonel Uri Rom, a forty-one-year-old Sabra, graduate of the U.S. school for armor at Fort Knox, Kentucky. One battalion of Shermans was left behind to guard Galilee. After doing the forty-seven miles to the border at a mad pace, Rom's brigade was held there for hours awaiting a political decision. Then orders came to attack Deir-Abu-Daif. Finding all other roads to the south and west blocked by dragon's teeth and mine fields, the brigade proceeded haltingly along a boulder-strewn wadi. When it got on the rear of the position at Umm Tut, it found a guard of only three M-47 tanks, promptly knocked them out, and rolled on south.

Confronting Rom's brigade at Tel Pit was its first acute problem: the Zababida valley entrance was defended by thirty-six M-48 tanks. The captain commanding the Israeli scout company was immediately killed by a recoilless rifle. Looking at the enemy front and concluding that it was too strong to crack, Rom tried to swing the brigade wide around the flank and was turned back in a running gun duel. He called in an air strike, which seemed effective: several tanks were burned; other crews quit their vehicles and fled for cover. (Here and elsewhere the Jordanian tankers made the mistake of carrying barrels of fuel strapped on the rear of the hulls; any missile hitting the barrel set the tank ablaze.) Darkness came and Rom broke off the fight. At midnight he tried again, hitting straight forward with all tanks dressed in twin columns, supported by fire from the 105-mm. batteries. The enemy crews had returned to their vehicles, and there was a big shoot. Most of the resistance was crushed by Rom's two platoons of Centurions. In forty-five minutes the brigade was across the valley.

Deploying at around 0200 Wednesday to attack the town of Tubas, the brigade found—when the scene was fully illuminated—that the Jordanians had fled. Rom continued on toward Nablus, with the mission of securing the high ground and blocking the two roads to the Jordan Valley. The scout troop ran on ahead to get a feel of the Nablus situation, and still short of the city, set up a blocking position, reinforced by a company of AMX tanks. Rom by then was weighing two messages, one from higher command, say-

Unopposed, an Israeli convoy winds down a road in the Syrian hills to a line of destroyed gun emplacements. For nearly two decades Israeli border settlements in the fertile valley (background) north of the Sea of Galilee were at the mercy of these Arab guns. Across the valley rise the more peaceful hills of a noncombatant neighbor, Lebanon.

When the fighting stopped on Saturday, June 10, the Syrian heights bore witness to the intensity of the final thrust. Shelled-out gun nests and demobilized armor pockmarked the rugged countryside. At right, an Israeli casualty is given plasma by an army medic, grimy from the dust of battle. Opposite, an overturned Syrian tank serves as a backdrop for two frolicking kittens, oblivious to the surrounding wreckage.

ing: "Fifty tanks in Nablus," and one from the commander of his reconnaissance group: "I have POW's; they say there is no force in Nablus." He decided to barrel straight in.

As his lead vehicles entered the city from one side—to the loud cheers of a populace that mistook his soldiers for Algerians—the first Jordanian Patton tanks (there were forty-one altogether) moved into the outskirts on the other side. By a stroke of luck, or genius, Rom had already turned the AMX company; it was looping northward around the city and would come in on the rear of the Pattons. He had already positioned his two infantry battalions on two hills to the east. His trap was set, and the Jordanian armor walked in.

The battle for Nablus raged from 1100 until 1600 on 7 June, and when it ended, seventeen Jordanian Pattons had been destroyed, mainly by AMX fire, and the others had been abandoned. Rom checked his own force; three tanks had been hit, not one had been destroyed. The brigade lost six men killed and forty-two wounded, most of them hit coming through the olive fields to the west of the city. On the following morning, Thursday, Rom got a hurry call to return to the Huleh Valley.

In two days, Israeli infantry and armor thrust deep into Syria's Golan hills, securing a buffer zone northeast of the Sea of Galilee. Clockwise, from above, are: a vehicle being hit, photographed through a tank's periscope; Israeli troops and a half-track in movement; an Israeli gun firing; a Syrian tank at the moment it has been hit.

At 0700 on Friday, 9 June, General Eleazar got orders from Chief of Staff General Rabin that he should attack Syria. From that moment he rushed, fearing only that a cancellation would come.

Composing a sufficient force in a hurry was a larger problem than drafting a crash plan. At hand were only one infantry brigade and two battalions of armor that had not fought against Jordan. He had risked Galilee and the Huleh area on this handful of troops, even though three Syrian brigades—the 11th, 8th, and 19th—with one battalion of armor apiece, were in the trenches fronting the Golan Plateau. Two other brigades were in support.

Several things were clear in Eleazar's mind. Some of the troops driving back from the Jordan West Bank would have to be used over again. The breakthrough would have to be made on a very narrow front. And since small forces would be attacking straight up steep ridges in daylight against rock-walled fortifications, the assault could not be made at all without large help from the air.

Eleazar decided he would try to crack the Syrian line with two brigades, the armored outfit back from Nablus and a somewhat fresher brigade of infantry that would move in half-tracks. This was the Golani Brigade, all regulars, commanded by Colonel Elfrat Yona, forty years old, a rather large and undramatic soldier with an impassive face, an honor graduate at Fort Leavenworth in 1963. East of Dan, south of Banias, the two columns would

124

first advance upward along two twisting dirt roads little more than one-half mile apart. Once the crust was broken, the infantry brigade would peel off to the north and south to exploit the situation and mop up. The armor would move northeast to get on the ridge line and then advance south along the high ground. It would be slow, tedious, and dangerous work, for the slopes below the trenches were sown with dragon's teeth and mines, and the wire entanglements were very broad.

Colonel Yona and his infantry brigade were ready to go by 0745, a few minutes after receiving the warning order. But they had to mark time until just before noon, waiting for the armored brigade to finish its forced march out of Jordan. However, the infantrymen could not proceed leisurely to their line of departure; they were under artillery fire throughout the two-and-one-half-hour move from Kiryat Shmone. Since Israel's fighter bombers were already attacking the Syrian gun bases, the Arab shelling was highly erratic.

On the Syrian side of the Huleh Valley the first ridges rise so sharply that one ascends from below sea level to more than one thousand feet above it in the first mile and one-half. And there is no cover against observation from the heights. A pimply hill, Givat Haem, is the last Israeli outpost next to the border. Azaziat, the westernmost Syrian redoubt, rises still higher off its flank, at a distance of three long city blocks, its crown peaked with a concrete turret, the hub of a system of basalt-walled trenches, bunkers, and pillboxes. It is an ugly scene, black and desolate.

Less than one mile to the east, commanding both hills and the valley, rises the Syrian fortress of Tel Fahar, seventy meters higher, also formed of volcanic rock. It is a three-pronged ridge, with the highest ground in the center, but with the defensive system spread over all three fingers. This whole fortification occupies about six acres. The works, including the covered communications trenches and sleeping bunkers, were built to withstand the heaviest bombing, and indeed, there is not one crater to be found on Tel Fahar. Just below the main fire trench begins a belt of mines and barbed-wire entanglements one hundred meters broad.

Here was the decisive battlefield of the Syrian fight, attacked by the two Israeli brigades at 1145 on Friday. Five tanks stopped at Givat Haem to provide covering fire as the tanks and half-tracks raced on to subdue Azaziat. The point-to-point struggle up the slope from there on is not to be covered in detail; it was all painfully slow going, with much fire and little movement, as the vehicles bent around the rock outcroppings, looking for any line where the tracks would hold.

The drawing above, made by General S. L. A. Marshall, shows the Syrian border strong point of Azaziat. Opposite, a photograph taken after the cease-fire shows a damaged section of Quneitra the day after it was taken by Israeli troops. In the picture below, a blindfolded Syrian sniper is brought in by his captors

126

Text continued on page 131.

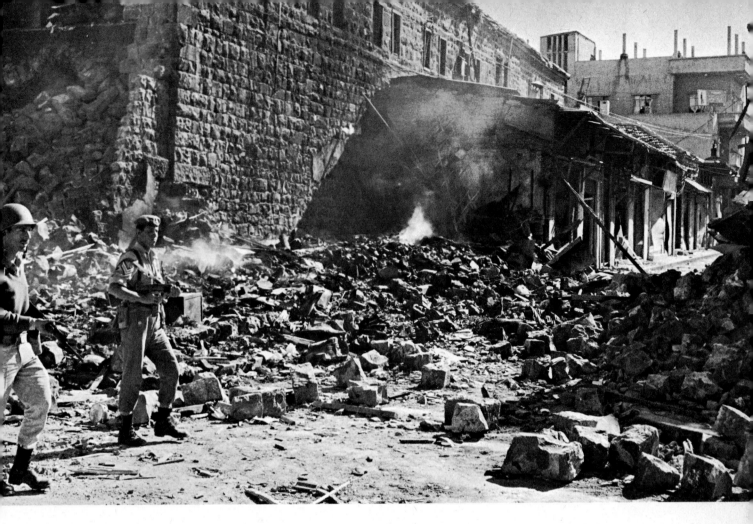

Among the most tragic victims of any war are those left homeless in its wake. The Israeli occupation of Jordan's West Bank on June 7 sent thousands of Arabs fleeing across the river to Jordanian-held territory. To many it was a repeat of their flight from Palestine during Israel's fight for independence in 1948. Taking the few possessions they could carry, men, women, and children made their way to the Jordan River, where they forded the waters at shallow points or crossed on the remains of the demolished Allenby Bridge near Jericho. At left, some refugees struggle through the current and the bridge's twisted spans, while others—like the mother, infant, and children above—await their turn to cross. At top right, an old woman is carried across the bridge on the back of a young man. The ancient, careworn face of a young boy (lower right) reflects the hopelessness with which the refugees view their plight.

Not until 1530 were some of Yona's infantrymen standing on the slope directly below Tel Fahar, ready for the last hard trial. There were only two companies now, totaling less than two hundred soldiers. The half-tracks got only as far as the lower side of the belt of mines and wire. There the company that had closed from the left, or south, side of the slope had seven half-tracks hit and knocked out. They could have climbed no higher in any case. The riflemen had to do it alone, crawling upward on their bellies along the slight creases of the ridge, or bounding from rock to rock.

Wiggling up that slope, the front files took more than an hour to reach the first Syrian fire trench on the military crest—a distance of only one hundred fifty meters. And some did not make it. In one company, only eight men were still up and going when the fight for the trenches began. All members of the wire-cutting party were hit before they could start. The eight who made it out of the one company were led by Major Alex Krinsky; still in the trench, he was killed seconds later by a rifle bullet. The battalion commander, Lieutenant Colonel Moshe Klein, had been shot from his half-track one mile before reaching the hill; he came on afoot, worked his way up to the center of the Syrian position, and there was shot dead. The artillery observer who accompanied Klein had heard noises behind him on the forward slope; he jumped that way, saw a group of four Syrians rushing to close the gap through which the attackers were entering, killed them with his Uzi, then rushed back to find Klein lying dead. One company commander was killed in front of the hill while standing in a half-track, directing his men. Another company commander, swinging wide to the north with the aim of coming in on the Syrian rear, was shot dead before he could get halfway. One hour after the fight started, the companies were under second lieutenants, with no channel to higher command.

Colonel Yona was rushing forward to restore communications. Dispatching his second-in-command to take charge of all units fighting south of the hill, he went for Tel Fahar, to take over. By the time he got there, thirty-seven Israeli dead and eighty-two wounded had paid the price for Tel Fahar. As Yona had guessed, the initial force had been wholly used up. His second battalion was coming on to continue the action.

The fight for Tel Fahar ended just before dark; only a few sniper rounds were heard after 1800. When Tel Fahar fell, the bottom dropped out of Syria's defensive wall and out of the Syrian army as well. That collapse was speeded by a radio announcement in Damascus that Quneitra had been captured by Israel's army. This was said in order to capture the ear of the United Nations—six hours before Eleazar's troops got anywhere near the city. Its unexpected effect as to put the whole Syrian army to flight.

Other moves were made by Eleazar to mop up the wedge of Syria, with Quneitra at its point, that Israel intended to hold for a time, but they were merely tidying-up exercises. The war against Syria had ended at Tel Fahar. So had the shortest conflict of the decade.

When the reserves stacked arms a few days later, and with their friends in the standing force, looked back, not exultantly but with a rightful pride in the achievement of their arms, they told one another that superior shooting accounted for the smash victory. But as did their civilian neighbors, they also spoke of "the miracle." Many things about the way they did it transcended technical explanation and mortal understanding.

Confused and frightened, a tearful Arab boy, his family leaving the Jewish Quarter of Jerusalem's Old City, learns what it is to become a refugee.

When Israel mobilized for the June 1967 war, several army reserve units reported that *more* than one hundred per cent of their members had responded to the call to arms. A number of middle-aged men, it seems, refusing to acknowledge the forty-nine-year-old age limit for reservists, had shown up.

The dedication of its fighting men has thrice in two decades forged victory for the Israeli army and salvation for the Israeli nation. Yet that dedication does not provide the Israeli soldier with the information required to set a mine, drop a bomb, shoot a gun, or fire a grenade. It does not teach the Israeli officer strategic principles, military judgment, or—and this is of incalculable importance in the Israeli army—the essentials of successful improvisation. Dedication may provide the will, but the army implements the will and turns it into a way to win wars and keep the state of Israel alive.

Because it is so small and isolated and its enemies are so large and threatening, Israel maintains military forces of a size disproportionate to the country's population, which is about 2,700,000. The army of roughly 289,000 men and women is not a standing army: only a small cadre of leaders are "regulars"; the rest are citizen-soldiers. To keep the large reserve force in combat readiness has been the principal challenge to military leaders, and they have met the challenge by developing an imaginative, common-sense system of training and maintenance that is unique.

Virtually all of Israel's eighteen-year-old males are inducted into the army for a period of two and a half years. As a rule, physical and mental handicaps are grounds for exemption only when the disability is virtually complete. Deferments are given only to persons whose work is clearly in the national interest and who have demonstrated leadership abilities. Young women are also called up for military duty, although the Women's Army Corps may accept only about twenty-five per cent

of the eligibles. The girls are trained to do almost everything the men are taught to do, including use of weapons.

In the United States Army, inductees are given a rigorous "basic training" that lasts thirteen weeks of the two-year service period. In the Israeli army the entire two and a half years is devoted to basic training. Soldiers are taught to use weapons, they engage in hard combat exercises and scouting missions, and they are simultaneously instructed in Hebrew, history, geography, and a special skill. For this reason, the thirty-month training period has become an important positive force in the non-military life of Israel. Composed of peoples from eighty different countries as alien in culture as Holland and Yemen, Israel has made the army its great equalizer and melder. Inasmuch as military service is truly universal, and inasmuch as all officers are drawn from the ranks, newcomers to the nation are exposed to a truly democratic system, and they emerge from the army with at least the foundation for a trade and further education.

From the beginning of training to the end, the army tends to place the soldier on his own as much as possible—much more than do most armies. Thus the Israeli fighting man develops into an independent sort, able to fend for himself if need be, inclined to improvise when improvisation is called for. Yet there seems to be no problem with discipline: the Israeli soldier follows orders. That he does so challenges many concepts of military discipline as old as warfare itself. The army spends very little time, for instance, in parade drill. Officers and men are generally on a first name basis and wear the same uniforms. When not in the field, where dress is casual, the army shines like any other. The military salute may or may not be given at any given time—it is a matter more of mood than of manual.

The Israeli army believes that leaders should

lead, not push, and in actual combat it loses a very high percentage of them. Nevertheless, the system pays off: the men seem to admire and take inspiration from the leaders up front and try doubly hard to become officers themselves.

Combining traditional military doctrines with common sense, Israeli military directives for leaders are easily learned and logically applied. A few of the most effectively applied rules include:

When your orders have not gotten through, assume what they must be.

When in doubt, strike.

Keep up the pressure until your troops are worn down, but when they are near exhaustion, pull back and have them rest.

Supplies are on the way; do not wait for them; they will catch up with you.

Keep your sense of humor.

The battle will never go as you planned it. Improvise.

Surprise is your most effective weapon.

Risk, risk, risk.

When an Israeli youth completes his thirty months of active service (generally forty-two months if he is an officer), he remains in the reserves until his forty-ninth year. As a rule, he reports one day each month for a brief refresher course in weaponry, field work, and general principles and gives from two weeks to a month each year to more intensive retraining.

Understandably, a citizen-soldier cannot always maintain the sharpened faculties, the level of efficiency, and the flexibility of the army regulars; and this can be especially serious for officers—as was demonstrated during the 1956 Sinai campaign. To help compensate for this and to increase the reserve officer's improvisational abilities, the army has developed a special series of exercises for the period of active duty. The series includes a variety of assignments, all calculated to catch the officer

off guard. Consequently, the regular staff does everything it can to do just that.

Here is a characteristic assignment: The newly arrived reserve brigade commander is taken out into the field with a full staff, communications equipment, and all necessary armor. Given a specific objective—capture of a well-protected town, for instance—he is asked to come up with a plan within two days. Made available to him are all maps, all reconnaissance and personnel, and as much consultation with the high command as he feels is necessary. The brigade is sent on its way, and on schedule, the officer delivers the plan. At that moment he is told that the brigade has been stopped at X, a fortified pass, that the enemy has moved all his facilities to point Y, behind a ridge, and that everything, therefore, has changed. There is no time for reconnaissance, but new maps are made available to him, and he is told that he has a half-hour to determine which way to dispatch his men, who are—remember—still engaged at X. Thirty minutes later he arrives back with his new battle plan, only to have it thrown into the wastebasket. The enemy, he is told, has struck and destroyed half the Israeli brigade, forcing the other half into Z, a valley, and has moved its major fortifications to a mountain overlooking the valley. No maps, no talk; he must attack that mountainside; he must say *now* how he is going to go about it.

Obviously, some brigade commanders go to pieces under the strain and are unable to come up with any thought other than retreat. Some suggest the obvious. But a few are both imaginative and logical. The army's aim, it goes without saying, is to ensure that the officers leading men under actual combat conditions will be those with the greatest natural or acquired strengths. As the army has demonstrated more convincingly in 1967 than ever before, the real and the ideal in Israeli military operations are not very far apart.

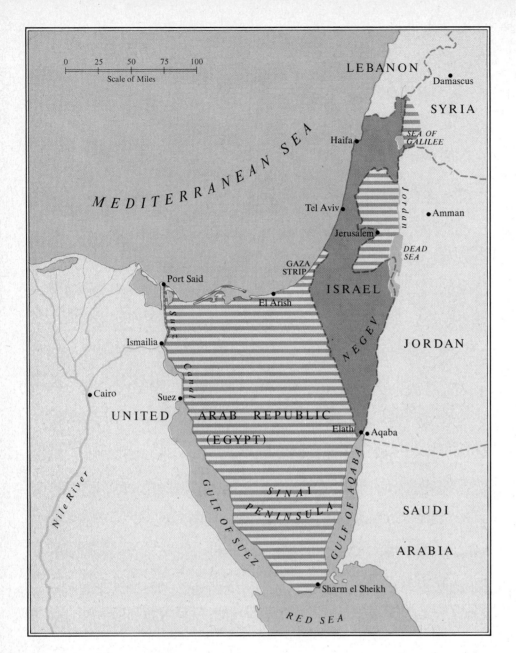

When acceptance of a final cease-fire halted fighting on June 10, Israel occupied a land area more than three times her own size (striped shading on the map at left). Israeli troops had penetrated on three fronts, taking the Syrian heights above the Sea of Galilee; the West Bank of the Jordan, including the Old City of Jerusalem; and the entire Sinai Peninsula in Egypt. With these areas as a bargaining point, Israel hoped to protect her frontiers from the kind of harassment that precipitated the June, 1967, war.

Israel's exhilaration following its swift victory was tempered by the cost of the triumph. More than seven hundred men had died, and in a country of only two and a half million, that is enough to affect every community. At right, a young woman visits the Tel Aviv military cemetery on the Sunday after the end of the war. Flowers of the season and rocks of ages share the new gravestone below.

*When the Israeli soldier at left re-
turned to his home on the kibbutz
of Gadot, he found that his family
also had been under fire. (North
of the Sea of Galilee, Gadot had
been almost constantly shelled by
the Syrians.) As the womenfolk
and another soldier look on, the
exhausted veteran pauses to talk
to his son before cleansing himself
of the battlefield's dust and mud.*

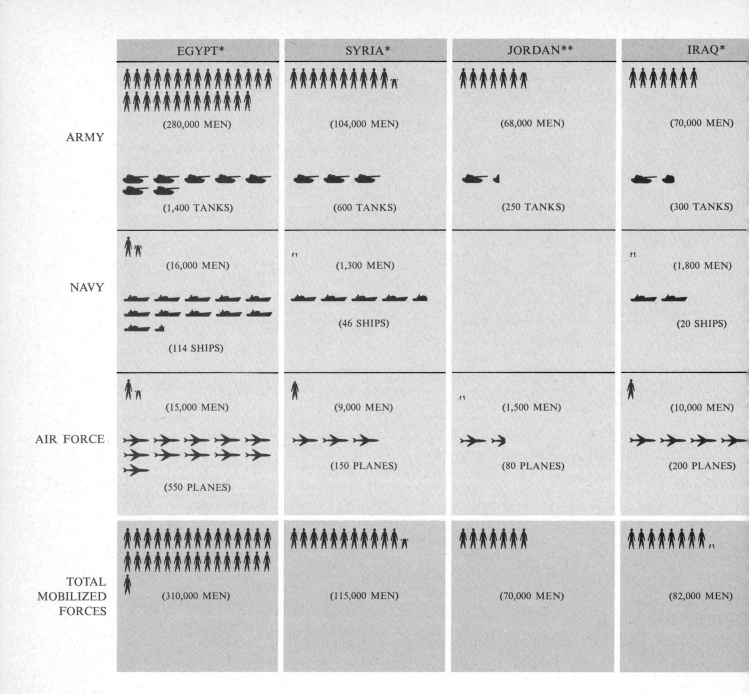

	EGYPT*	SYRIA*	JORDAN**	IRAQ*
ARMY	(280,000 MEN)	(104,000 MEN)	(68,000 MEN)	(70,000 MEN)
	(1,400 TANKS)	(600 TANKS)	(250 TANKS)	(300 TANKS)
NAVY	(16,000 MEN)	(1,300 MEN)		(1,800 MEN)
	(114 SHIPS)	(46 SHIPS)		(20 SHIPS)
AIR FORCE	(15,000 MEN)	(9,000 MEN)	(1,500 MEN)	(10,000 MEN)
	(550 PLANES)	(150 PLANES)	(80 PLANES)	(200 PLANES)
TOTAL MOBILIZED FORCES	(310,000 MEN)	(115,000 MEN)	(70,000 MEN)	(82,000 MEN)

The Middle East: Opposing Forces

The history of the arms race in the Middle East is, to some extent, a history of Cold War rivalries. Since World War II the United States, committed to the containment of Communism, has been vying with the Soviet Union for spheres of influence in the strategically and economically vital areas of the Middle East. While both nations have attempted to woo the oil-rich Arab countries by political and economic means, the balance of power in that area has become increasingly contingent upon military support. Thus, the West sells arms to Jordan, Lebanon, and Saudi Arabia, countering Soviet aid to Egypt, Syria, and Iraq. The situation is further complicated by intra-Arab rivalries and Arab hostility toward Israel.

The extension of the Cold War to the Middle East began in earnest shortly after NATO was established in 1949 to counteract the growing military capabilities of the Soviet Union. Since then the United States has been pumping military strength into NATO's easternmost member, Turkey, and neighboring Iran. As an added buffer, the United States signed a military pact with Iraq in 1954 and was soon supplying arms secretly to Saudi Arabia. Fearing Iraq's new power as a challenge to his leadership of the Arab world, Egypt's Gamal Abdel Nasser began to negotiate for Soviet

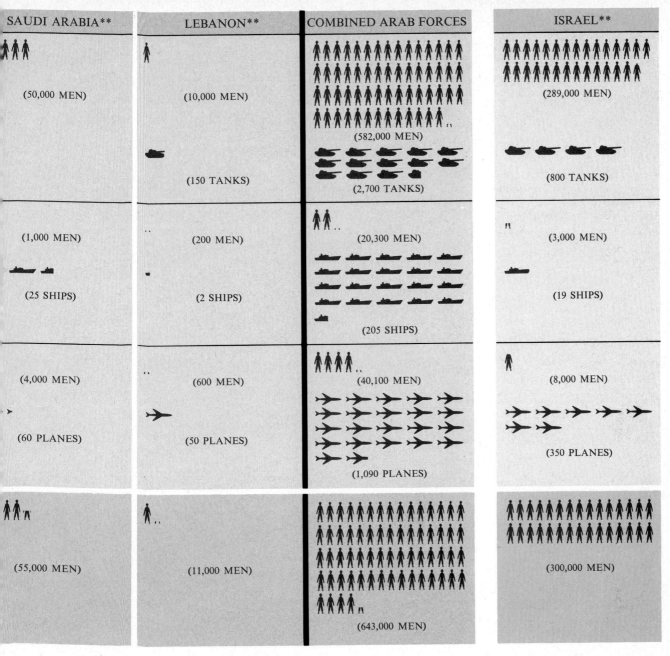

SAUDI ARABIA**	LEBANON**	COMBINED ARAB FORCES	ISRAEL**
(50,000 MEN)	(10,000 MEN)	(582,000 MEN)	(289,000 MEN)
	(150 TANKS)	(2,700 TANKS)	(800 TANKS)
(1,000 MEN)	(200 MEN)	(20,300 MEN)	(3,000 MEN)
(25 SHIPS)	(2 SHIPS)	(205 SHIPS)	(19 SHIPS)
(4,000 MEN)	(600 MEN)	(40,100 MEN)	(8,000 MEN)
(60 PLANES)	(50 PLANES)	(1,090 PLANES)	(350 PLANES)
(55,000 MEN)	(11,000 MEN)	(643,000 MEN)	(300,000 MEN)

= 10,000 MEN

= 200 TANKS

= 10 SHIPS

= 50 PLANES

*Countries receiving Soviet
military equipment.

**Countries receiving Western
military equipment.

aid. Israel—in turn alarmed by Egypt's growing strength and Nasser's 1956 seizure of the Suez Canal—appealed for Western aid. France and Britain agreed to supply Israel with military hardware. The United States' policy of nonintervention in the subsequent Suez crisis, however, weakened Arab confidence in Western unity.

In 1957 the United States moved to strengthen her position by promising Middle Eastern countries protection from aggression under the Eisenhower Doctrine. Almost immediately, Jordan enlisted American aid to prevent an impending Egyptian take-over. A year later Lebanon followed suit, as the new Egypt-Syria union—supported by Soviet military aid—threatened to undermine the Lebanese government. The take-over of Iraq by anti-Western forces intensified the crisis, and the United States rushed arms—and men—to Lebanon. Then, caught in the embarrassing position of supplying weapons to Israel's border enemies, the United States began—in secret—providing Israel with the means for her defense.

With the major powers thus aligned, Israel watched as Cold War tactics strengthened her foes and threatened her existence. By June, 1967, the relative strength of Israel and her six surrounding Arab neighbors was as indicated in the chart above.

Chronology

2000–1750 B.C.	Abraham brings worship of one God from Mesopotamia to Palestine.
1700–1600	Hebrew descendants of Abraham, driven by famine, enter Egypt, where they are enslaved.
1300–1200	Jews flee Egypt; during 40 years wandering in the desert, Moses receives Ten Commandments.
1200–1100	Hebrew people return to Palestine, establish a kingdom.
1000–900	Reigns of David and Solomon.
586	Jews' First Temple in Jerusalem destroyed by invading Babylonians; many Jews taken into captivity.
	This exile, plus voluntary emigration of other Jews in succeeding centuries, leads to Diaspora (dispersion).
538	Returning from Babylonian captivity, Jews begin building their Second Temple.

167	Judas Maccabaeus re-establishes Jewish kingdom in Palestine.
63	Rome conquers Palestine.
19	Herod the Great, a Roman puppet, enlarges the Second Temple.
A.D. 30	Jesus of Nazareth is crucified.
70	Rome crushes a Jewish rebellion.
	Temple is destroyed, and Jews are again dispersed. (Wailing Wall in modern Jerusalem is all that remains of the Second Temple.)
570	Mohammed is born.
614	Persians invade Palestine.
622	Mohammed flees from Medina to Mecca, where he organizes the commonwealth of Islam.
632–738	Moslems, Mohammed's followers, conquer North Africa.

638	Arabs capture Jerusalem.
715	Moslems conquer Spain.
732	Moslem expansion into Europe stopped at Battle of Tours.
1099	First Crusade to free Palestine from Moslems results in establishment of French feudal kingdom.
1187	Egyptians capture Jerusalem.
1192	Third Crusade wins Christian access to Jerusalem for three years.
1229	Sixth Crusade gains ten-year access to Jerusalem and Bethlehem for Christians.
1270	Eighth Crusade, last of true expeditions, fails to reach Jerusalem.
1290	Jews expelled from England.
1306	Jews expelled from France.
1492	Jews expelled from Spain by Ferdinand and Isabella.
1496	Jews expelled from Portugal.
1517	Turks capture Palestine, Egypt, Arabia, and Syria.
1798	Napoleon, having seized Egypt, fails in attempt to capture Palestine.
1860–1900	Communities of European Jews established in Palestine.
1869	Suez Canal is opened.
1875	Britain assumes control of Suez Canal.
1881	Russian Jews subjected to pogroms; many emigrate to U.S., Argentina, and Palestine.
1894	Conviction for treason of Captain Dreyfus leads to overt anti-Semitism in France.
1897	Dr. Theodor Herzl, at first Zionist Congress in Basel, Switzerland, announces aim of creating a Jewish homeland in Palestine.
1911	Permanent housing is completed at Degania for first cooperative communal settlement in Palestine (model for future kibbutzim).
1917	In a declaration issued to Lord Rothschild on November 2, by Foreign Secretary Arthur James Balfour, Britain promises to help establish a national home for the Jewish people in Palestine.
1918	British defeat Turks in Palestine at end of World War I.
1922	League of Nations makes Palestine a British mandate.
1922–	During British rule, Arab extremists and

1937	Jewish terrorists exchange attacks.
1933	Anti-Semitism in Germany and Poland leads to renewed Jewish emigration to Palestine. (1931, Jews constituted 17% of population of Palestine; 1940, 33% population.)
1937	British Royal Commission finds the mandate unworkable and recommends the partition of Palestine between Arabs and Jews.
1939–1945	Six million European Jews killed in Nazi concentration camps.
1948	State of Israel proclaimed on May 14; Arab nations invade Israel.
1949	War of independence ends on January 7. Israel receives additional 2,380 square miles of territory under armistice agreement. U.N. patrols Israeli-Arab borders.
1952	Military coup overthrows Egypt's King Farouk; Nasser comes to power.
1956	After U.S. withdraws financial support for Egypt's Aswan Dam in July, Nasser nationalizes the Suez canal.
	Israeli forces invade Sinai on October 29; British and French paratroopers seize Suez Canal on November 5. United Nations enforces a cease-fire; French and British relinquish Suez.
1957	Israel withdraws to 1949 armistice lines. United Nations troops stationed in Gaza.
	Under Eisenhower doctrine, U.S. offers support to non-Communist countries in the Middle East.
1958	Nasser proclaims United Arab Republic (Egypt and Syria) in January.
	July revolt in Iraq overthrows pro-Western government. To bolster anti-Communist governments, U.S. marines land in Lebanon, British troops land in Jordan.
1961	Syria withdraws from U.A.R.
1961–1965	Israeli-Egyptian border remains quiet; snipers' gunfire exchanged in Jerusalem; cultivation of disputed land areas leads to sporadic firing on the Syrian border.
	Arab attempts are made to start diverting the waters of the Jordan, while Israel works on diversion of its Jordan water to the Negev.
1962	After harassment of her fishing boats on the Sea of Galilee, Israel conducts a reprisal raid against Syria.

1966   In reprisal for Syrian terrorist action; Israel conducts raid against Jordanian village on November 13 and levels forty houses. U.N. censures Israel.

1967

April 6   Israel conducts a reprisal against Syrian raids; six Syrian jets destroyed.

May 15   Armies of Egypt, Syria, Jordan, and Iraq begin to mobilize.

May 18   Egyptian President Nasser requests withdrawal of United Nations Emergency Forces from U.A.R.-Israeli border; sends in Egyptian forces.

May 20   U.N. Secretary-General U Thant confers with Nasser in Cairo in attempt to settle crisis. Israel calls up reserves.

May 23   Nasser announces blockade of Gulf of Aqaba.

May 24   U.N. Security Council called into session. Russian delegate blames crisis on "Israeli extremists."

May 26   France proposes four-power action to end crisis.

           Nasser asserts that, in event of war, Egypt's aims would be "the destruction of Israel."

May 30   Egypt and Jordan sign military alliance, completing Arab encirclement of Israel.

May 31   Israeli plants close down; workers don military uniforms.

June 1   General Moshe Dayan named Israeli Defense Minister.

June 2   U.S. and Great Britain propose declaration asserting international status of Gulf of Aqaba.

           Egypt threatens to close Suez Canal to nations breaking Aqaba blockade.

June 3   Israel announces to U.N. Security Council its determination "to make a stand on the Gulf of Aqaba."

June 4   Nasser warns that any declaration by the maritime powers asserting Gulf of Aqaba's international status would be considered "a preliminary to an act of war."

June 5   Egypt, Jordan, Syria, Iraq, Algeria, the Sudan, and Kuwait declare war on Israel.

           Saudi Arabia, Morocco, Yemen, and Tunisia pledge support.

Nasser says Arabs seek to "eliminate the shadow of Zionism from Palestine."

Dayan disclaims territorial ambitions for Israel.

U.S. takes neutral position, with commitment to support the territorial integrity of all Middle East nations.

France suspends shipment of military supplies to Middle East.

Arab nations threaten stoppage of oil flow to any Western powers aiding Israel.

Security Council is deadlocked over cease-fire resolution.

War begins, 8:00 A.M. Middle Eastern Time

Israeli planes destroy Arab air bases in Egypt, Jordan, Syria, and Iraq.

Syrian, Jordanian, and Iraqi planes retaliate in strikes against Israeli air bases.

Israeli land forces take Rahfa and Khan Yunis in Gaza Strip. Tank columns advance thirty miles into Sinai, capturing El Arish.

Israelis and Jordanians exchange fire along Jerusalem's dividing line.

June 6   Nasser charges U.S. and Great Britain with air war intervention; breaks diplomatic ties with U.S.; closes Suez Canal.

U.S. and Great Britain deny Nasser's charge; U.S. breaks diplomatic relations with Cairo.

Israeli Premier Levi Eshkol appeals to Soviet Union to help establish peace.

Soviet Union labels Israel aggressor; demands withdrawal of Israeli troops from Egypt.

Kuwait and Iraq suspend oil shipments to U.S. and Great Britain. Algeria nationalizes Western oil firms.

Syria and Iraq break diplomatic ties with U.S. and Great Britain. Algeria breaks ties with U.S.

Britain suspends arms shipments to Middle East; urges general arms embargo of all belligerents.

Security Council unanimously adopts cease-fire resolution.

Israeli tank columns advance toward Suez Canal on three major fronts: (1) through El Arish toward Kantara in north; (2) through Abu Agueila along central route toward Ismailia; (3) to Queisima on southern route. Other columns advance to Kuntilla farther south.

Israelis capture Jordanian cities of Jenin, Kalkilia, and Ramallah; take high ground north of Jerusalem.

Syria attacks and shells northern Israeli border settlements.

June 7   Israel accepts U.N. cease-fire provided other belligerents comply. Jordan accepts cease-fire.

Egypt rejects cease-fire.

Soviet Union threatens diplomatic break if Israel does not observe cease-fire.

France proposes international agreement for Aqaba similar to that of Dardanelles in Turkey.

Britain urges Israel to halt military action to pave way for peace settlement.

Jordan accuses Israel of violating cease-fire.

Yemen, the Sudan, and Mauritania break diplomatic relations with U.S. Lebanon recalls ambassador without severing relations.

Israeli forces take Gaza; gain control of Gaza Strip.

Israeli units sweep across Sinai, advancing within eighteen miles of Suez Canal in the north and reaching toward Mitla Pass in the south. Other forces capture Sharm-el-Sheikh at entrance to Gulf of Aqaba, breaking blockade at Strait of Tiran.

Israel proclaims victory on Sinai Peninsula.

Israeli forces capture Jordanian sector of Jerusalem; gain control of West Bank of

Jordan River; and defeat Jordanian army and accompanying Iraqi units. War ends on Jordanian front.

June 8   Egypt and Syria accept cease-fire.

Britain ends arms embargo to Middle East.

Mistaken Israeli attack on U.S. communications ship *Liberty* in Mediterranean kills thirty-four, wounds seventy-five.

Israel apologizes for mistaken attack on U.S. ship *Liberty*.

Israeli government releases tapes of Nasser-Hussein telephone conversation in which they discuss blaming the U.S. and Britain for air attacks.

After heavy fighting at Bir Gifgafa and Mitla pass in Sinai, Israelis block Egyptian escape routes across Suez Canal. In drive farther south, Israeli forces rout Egyptians after intense battle at Nakhl. War ends on Sinai front.

June 9   Nasser resigns as President of U.A.R.; National Assembly rejects resignation.

U Thant reactivates U.N. Observer Corps to oversee cease-fire.

Israel charges Syria with violation of cease-fire.

Pentagon initiates investigation of *Liberty* attack.

Israeli-Syrian border battle erupts in violation of cease-fire agreement. In thirty-hour battle, Israelis direct land and air attacks in direction of Damascus, gain control of heights near Sea of Galilee, and occupy border strip approximately twelve miles wide.

June 10   Israel offers compensation for loss of lives and damage in *Liberty* attack.

Soviet Union breaks diplomatic ties with Israel.

Israel and Syria agree to final cease-fire, 6:30 P.M. Middle Eastern time.

Fighting ends on Syrian front.

Israeli-Arab war ends, 6:30 P.M. Middle Eastern time.

ENDSHEETS: *The remarkable color photograph of the ancient lands of the Middle East in which the fighting took place was taken from five hundred miles above the earth, from Gemini II. Boundaries and place names have been superimposed.*

A NOTE ON THIS BOOK

This book was produced jointly by United Press International and American Heritage Publishing Co., Inc., under the following editorial direction: for United Press International, Roger Tatarian, Vice President and Editor, and Harold Blumenfeld, Executive Newspictures Editor; for American Heritage, Richard M. Ketchum, Editorial Director of the Book Division, and Irwin Glusker, Senior Art Director.

The staff for this book was as follows: Editor, Joseph L. Gardner; Art Director, John Conley; Copy Editor, Sandra L. Russell; Picture Editor, Laurie B. Platt; Assistant Editors, David Jacobs and Nancy Kelly; Editorial Assistants, Kathleen Fitzpatrick, Annette Jarman, John Levine, Janet Lloyd, Mary Elizabeth Wise.

Maps by Herbert S. Borst

The author: Brigadier General S. L. A. Marshall (Ret.) served in World War I, World War II and Korea and in the intervening years worked as a columnist and war correspondent. He has contributed articles to many leading magazines and served for years as military critic for the Detroit *News*. General Marshall's previous books include: *The American Heritage History of World War I, Blitzkrieg, Pork Chop Hill, Sinai Victory, Night Drop*, and *Battles in the Monsoon*.

Picture Credits: NASA, Front and back endsheets. UPI, 11 top and bottom. United Nations, 12. Charles Phelps Cushing, 13 top. UPI, 13 bottom, 14. Fred Ward—Black Star, 15. Pictorial Parade, 16, 17, 20–21. Anthony Howarth—Black Star, 24–25. UPI, 30–31, 36, 37, 45, 48–49, 60, 72–73. Franz Goess—Black Star, 78 top. Pictorial Parade, 78 bottom. UPI, 83 bottom, 84–85, 88–89 top and bottom. Pictorial Parade, 89 top. Anthony Howarth—Black Star, 91 top. Gamma-Pix, 91 bottom. Pictorial Parade, 110–11. Leonard Freed—Magnum, 112–13. Mark St. Gil—Black Star, 114, 115. UPI, 116–117. Mark St. Gil—Black Star, 119. Gamma Pix, 123. UPI, 124. Gamma-Pix, 124–125, 125. UPI, 127 top and bottom. Leonard Freed—Magnum, 129 top left and right. Micha Bar-Am and Cornell Capa—Magnum, Cover, 7, 16–17, 18, 34, 50–51, 57, 58–59, 62 top left, bottom right, 63 top and bottom, 66–67, 68 top and bottom, 70–71, 78–79, 81, 86–87, 94 through 105, 106, 107, 113 top and bottom, 120–21, 122, 135 top and bottom. Charles Harbutt—Magnum, 8–9, 10, 38 through 44, 47, 62 top right and bottom left, 63 bottom, 93, 128, 129 bottom, 130, 136. Israeli Government Press Office, Title page, 25, 26, 28, 29, 32, 33, 46, 55, 65, 74, 75, 76–77, 83 top, 90, 108, 118.

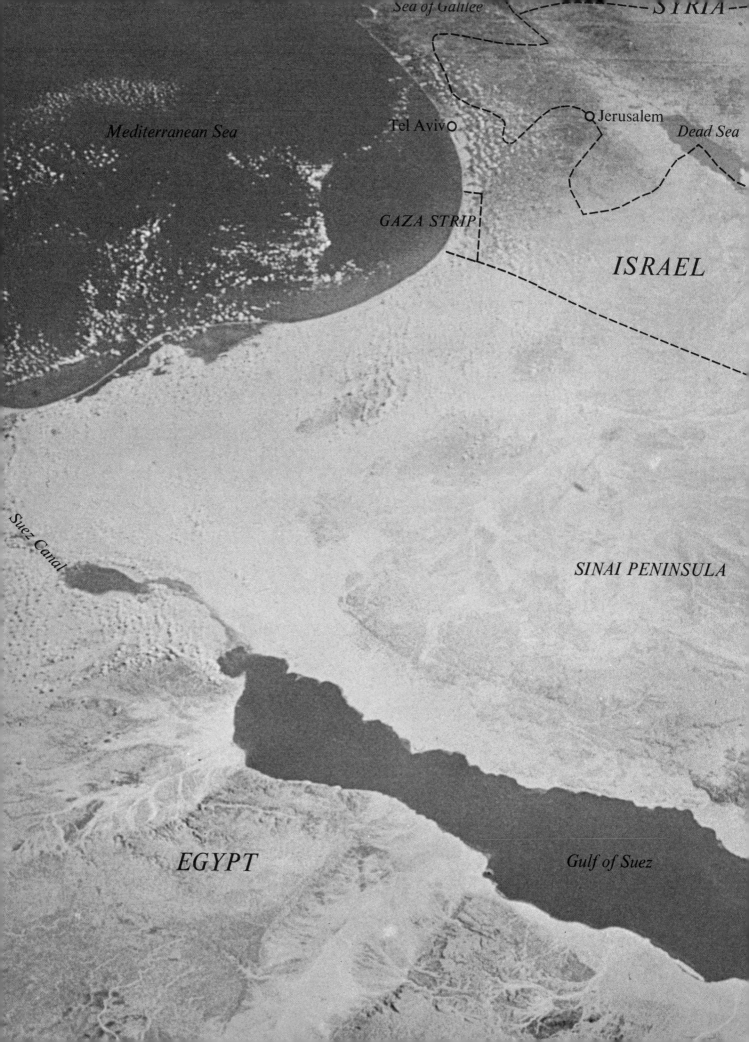